MAWLID AN NABAWI
A Critical Analysis of the Islamic Celebration

W0007561

Mufti Muhammad Khān Qādri

Translated & Annotated by
Muhammad Sājid Younus (Al Sultāni)

TRUE ISLAM PUBLICATIONS

MAWLID AN NABAWI
A Critical Analysis of the Islamic Celebration

Author: Mufti Muhammad Khān Qādri
Translated & Annotated: Muhammad Sājid Younus

Published by: TrueIslam Publications
Facebook: Trueislam Publications
Twittter: @shahswaar
Website: www.trueIslam.org.uk
Email: info@trueIslam.org.uk

Published in December 2015/Rabi ul Awwal 1437

ISBN: 978-0-9568965-4-4

A CIP catalogue record for this book is available in the British Library

Typeset: TrueIslam Media
Cover Design and Print: White Canvas

Contents

What is the Mawlid Gathering?

It is important from the outset to know that for Muslims, the Mawlid celebration or gathering is held for the blessed remembrance of the Prophet ﷺ, for remembering his ﷺ blessed life, his ﷺ perfections and ranks, remembering Allah's ﷻ greatest blessing in his guise, recounting the special events that occurred at the time of his ﷺ birth, taking out processions in joy, raising awareness of the commands of the pure Shariah, and performing nasheeds, sadaqah and other good acts.

In explaining the reality of the Mawlid, Imām Jalāl ud dīn Suyooti writes:

> Verily the reality of the Mawlid is the gathering of the people, the recitation of the Quran, the narrating of the ahadith that mention the Prophet's ﷺ birth, and then partaking in food that is available. These are the good acts upon which there is reward, because in them is the honour and respect of the Prophet ﷺ and display of happiness over his ﷺ arrival.
>
> *(Husn ul maqsid fi amal il mowlid)*

Molāna Shah Muhammad Salāmat ullah writes in *'Ishbā ul kalām fi ithbāt il mawlid wal qiyām'*:

> The reality of this good act is nothing save that in the month of Rabi ul Awwal, or any other month, the *fudalā,* ulema, pious and poor gather in a house at the invitation of a Muslim, or everyone congregates in a public place and there is a great gathering in which the parts of the Quran which mention the

1

Prophet's ﷺ greatness and perfections are recited. Similarly those authentic ahadith are narrated which mention his ﷺ blessed birth.'

(Ad durr ul Munazzam)

No one considers acts such as dancing or any other act that is contrary to Shariah to be permissible in these gatherings. If someone does believe such acts to be part of the Mawlid, then that is his misunderstanding. Such a person should recall the writings of the ulema. If some people do undertake such acts, they should reflect upon this, but for others to label the Mawlid and its gathering as a bid'ah and contrary to Shariah because of the actions of some people is also a clear transgression. No scholar to this day has ever claimed that because shoes are stolen from mosques, we should stop having mosques! Rather we should encourage the safeguarding of shoes and making provisions for them.

The Quran and the Mawlid Gathering

Now that we have determined what the Mawlid gathering is, let us proceed to ask whether all of these acts are proven by the Quran and Sunnah, or even the first generation of Muslims.

You will find that the Quran and Sunnah are honest witnesses to each and every part of these gatherings. Some instances are mentioned below:

Allah ﷻ Himself held the first gathering!

The Quran informs us that the first gathering of this kind was held by Allah ﷻ Himself. We are told that all its participants were prophets and the agenda of that gathering was the Prophet's ﷺ virtues and attributes. An oath was also taken by the prophets, to which Allah ﷻ Himself was witness:

> And, (O Beloved, recall) when Allah ﷻ took a firm covenant from the prophets: 'When I give you the Book and Wisdom, and then there comes to you the Messenger (who is exalted in glory above all and) who shall validate the Books you will have with you, you shall then, most certainly, believe in him and most surely help him.'
> Allah ﷻ said: 'Do you affirm, and on this (condition) hold fast to my heavy covenant?'
> All submitted: 'We affirm.'
> Allah ﷻ said: 'Bear witness then, and I am also with you amongst the witnesses.' *(Quran 3:81)*

This reveals that holding a gathering to remember the Prophet ﷺ is a divine sunnah (practice) and Allah ﷻ Himself organised the first such gathering. When was this held? Knowing that is beyond human capability!

No other messenger made his risāla a part of the declaration of faith (kalima)

When we study the teachings of the earlier prophets, we find that none of them mentioned their messengership in the *kalima* they taught their nations. Not one of the 313 messengers mentioned it; for example, Syeduna Nuh was a messenger but he taught '*Lā ilāha illallāhu Nuh Najeeh ullah*', Syeduna Ibraheem taught '*Lā ilāha illallāhu Ibraheem Khalill ullah*', Syeduna Ismaeel taught '*Lā ilāha illallāhu Ismaeel Zabeeh ullah*', Syeduna Musa taught '*Lā ilāha illallāhu Musa Kaleem ullah*', whilst Syeduna Isa taught '*Lā ilāha illallāhu Isa Ruh ullah*. It was only the Prophet ﷺ who mentioned his risāla in his kalima: '*Lā ilāha illallāhu Muhammad ur Rasool ullah.*'

This very verse explains the reason for this, as Allah ﷻ refers to all the other messengers as prophets and His ﷻ beloved as *rasool* (messenger). It was because of this distinction that none of the others mentioned their risāla in their kalima.

Mentioning Allah's ﷻ great blessing in the form of the Prophet ﷺ

The Quran, in many places, refers to the various, innumerable blessings bestowed upon human beings, stating:

> And He has given you everything that you asked Him for, and if you seek to number the favours of Allah, you will not be able to count them all. Indeed, man is highly unjust and extremely ungrateful. *(Quran 14:34)*

However, Allah ﷻ does not remind human beings of any of His favours, only His greatest favour, in the form of His beloved. Allah ﷻ said:

> Indeed, Allah bestowed a favour upon the believers when he raised up in their midst a messenger from among themselves, to convey

4

His messages unto them, and to cause them to grow in purity, and to impart unto them the divine writ as well as wisdom.

(Quran 3:164)

In another verse, He ﷻ denotes the Messenger and his Shariah as the most complete, most perfect and most final.

Today I have perfected your Dīn (Religion) for you, and have completed My Blessing upon you. *(Quran 5:3)*

Here, the words {I have completed my blessing upon you} are worthy of careful attention, as it is through these that Allah ﷻ announces that His most perfect and complete blessing is the Man of the Quran ﷺ and the Quran.

He ﷺ is Allah's ﷻ greatest Bounty and Mercy

In the above verse, the Quran calls the Prophet ﷺ the greatest blessing, in other places he ﷺ is Allah's ﷻ greatest Bounty and Mercy:

And, (O Esteemed Messenger), We have not sent you but as a mercy for all the worlds. *(Quran 21:107)*

A mercy for all of Allah's ﷻ creation means that the existence of all of creation is through and because of him ﷺ. When our very existence depends upon him ﷺ, can there be any other greater Bounty and Mercy for us?

In Sura Ahzāb, after describing him ﷺ as *Shāhid* (witness) *Mubasshir* (giver of glad tidings), *Nazeer* (warner), *Dā ee bi izn illah* (Caller to Allah) and *Sirāj um Muneer* (Light spreading Sun), it then commands:

O (Esteemed) Prophet! Surely, We have sent you as a Witness (to the truth and the creation), a Bearer of glad tidings and a Warner, And (as) an Inviter towards Allah by His command and as a Sun spreading Light. And give good news to the believers that there is for them Allah's great bounty. *(Quran 33: 45-47)*

Effectively, this verse informs the people that in granting such an esteemed prophet, He ﷻ has bestowed a great *fadhl* (Bounty) upon them!

Why is it the greatest Fadhl?

The Quran also reveals the reason why the Prophet ﷺ is the greatest *fadhl;* because Allah has bestowed the most *fadhl* on him. The Quran states this in the following verses:

> But that by your Lord's mercy (We have kept it intact. This) is indeed His mighty favour to you (and through you to your Ummah [Community]). *(Quran 17:87)*

Later, when mentioning the knowledge bestowed upon the Prophet ﷺ, it says:

> And has bestowed upon you all that knowledge which you did not possess. Mighty indeed is Allah's bounty on you. *(Quran 4:113)*

It was with him that the system of Prophethood and Messengership concluded, which in itself was a great *fadhl* of Allah upon creation. In Sura Ahzāb, verse 40, it is written:

> Muhammad is not the father of any of your men, but he is the Messenger of Allah and the Last of the Prophets. And Allah is the Perfect Knower of everything.

Allah's ﷻ command to express joy on every mercy and blessing

The Quran taught its followers that when they are apportioned any blessing, or His ﷻ Bounty and Mercy, they should express happiness, because His ﷻ Bounty and Mercy are better and greater than anything else.

> Say: 'With the bounty and mercy of Allah the Muslims should rejoice. This is far better than what that they amass.'
> *'(Quran 10:58)*

Every word of this Divine Command orders that when the mercy and bounty of Allah ﷻ is received, there should be an expression of happiness, because for a servant there is nothing better than Allah's ﷻ *fadhl* and kindness.

It is stated in Sura Ad Duhā (93:11):

> And proclaim (well) the bounties of your Lord.

The Quran also mentions that Syeduna Isa عليه السلام supplicated to be blessed with a table of food, and that he would celebrate its receipt as an Eid and happiness. The words of this beautiful supplication are:

> O our Lord, send us from heaven a table set, that there may be for us, the first and the last of us, an Eid (a solemn festival).
>
> *(Quran 5: 114)*

As the Prophet ﷺ is a great blessing, it is necessary for the ummah to remember and be grateful for this blessing. One way of doing this would be for the ummah to gather together and collectively praise and eulogise Him ﷺ for His great blessing, and spread awareness of the virtues and excellences of the Messenger He sent. Then, as awareness of his virtues and excellence increases, so too will people's gratitude towards Allah ﷻ for His blessing of such a prophet.

Some may claim that it is not correct to use this verse to prove the permissibility of the Mawlid gathering:

> Say 'With the bounty and mercy of Allah the Muslims should rejoice. This is far better than what that they amass'
>
> *(Quran 10 58)*[1]

However, the people of knowledge have used these verses of Sura Yunus to prove the permissibility of the Mawlid gathering, the full text is:

---

[1] For it has nothing to do with the arrival of the Prophet ﷺ.

O mankind! Surely, there has come to you an admonition from your Lord, and a cure for all those (diseases) which are (hidden) in the breasts. And it is guidance and mercy (too) for those who are blessed with faith. O people, has come to you from your Lord a Counsel, a Cure for what is in the Hearts, Guidance and a Mercy for all the believers. Say, with Allah's fadhl and mercy rejoice, (for) it is better than which you gather.' *(Quran 10: 57-58)*

These divine words unequivocally provide the principle that displaying happiness and joy upon the receipt of every *fadhl* and mercy of Allah ﷻ is a religious command. The Quran, Islam and all good things are *fadhl* from Allah ﷻ, and however much gratitude we show, it will always be insufficient. Furthermore, as the Prophet ﷺ is Allah's ﷻ greatest favour and *fadhl* upon creation - indeed he is the means and source of Allah's ﷻ *fadhl* and mercy - believers should display greater happiness over his arrival than all other things. The gathering of the Mawlid is one collective way of showing such gratitude.

Fadhl and Mercy not the Prophet ﷺ?

In rejecting this reasoning, some claim that the *fadhl* and mercy of Allah ﷻ stated here only refer to Islam and the Quran and cannot be taken as referring to the Prophet ﷺ.

Before evaluating this claim, we should first understand why this verse was revealed:

The reason for this verse's revelation

If we look at the reasons for this verse's revelation, we find two reasons:

1) To highlight that spiritual goodness is better than physical goodness.
2) To reveal that one should not be pleased with spiritual goodness in itself, but should be happy because it comes from Allah ﷻ.

8

The Shaykh of the exegisists *(mufassireen)*, Imām Fakhruddin Ar Rāzi explained these verses in great detail and, after mentioning the two reasons above, revealed that these verses are clear proof of prophethood. Take a look at a synopsis of his discussion:

Issue 1: There are two ways to prove prophethood, one that a person claims prophethood and then performs a miracle, after which he will be considered a messenger from Allah ﷻ. In explaining this, this same Sura states: {*This Qur'an is not such as could be devised without (the Revelation of) Allah. Rather, (it) validates those (Books) which have been (revealed) before it, and is an exposition of whatever (Allah) has written (on the Tablet or in the commandments of Shariah). There is not even an iota of doubt in its (veracity). It is from the Lord of all the worlds. Do they say: 'The Messenger has fabricated it himself'? Say: 'Then bring forth any (one) Sura (chapter) like it, and call on (for your help) all you can besides Allah if you are truthful.*}

(Quran 10: 37-38)

The second way is for us to determine true creed and righteous deeds. The result will be that every belief and act that frees us from the *duniya* and turns us to the Ākhirah is pious, and any act leading to the opposite is not righteous. To determine such a thing requires a person who is perfect, strong willed, and with an enlightened soul and an elevated character that is able to transform the deficient creation into perfection. Such a person is a prophet. Furthermore, as there are different levels of human deficiency, it is obvious that there will be various levels of prophets.

When this purpose has become known, I (Rāzi) state that in the earlier verse, Allah ﷻ demonstrated the authenticity of the prophethood of Muhammad ﷺ through a miracle. In this verse, 57, He ﷻ proves the veracity of his prophethood in the second way and thereby reveals the reality of prophethood and defines its essence. The second way is undoubtedly better, grander and more complete than the first way.

Issue 2: It should be noted that here (in verse 57) Allah ﷻ mentions 4 attributes of the Quran:

- Counsel from Allah ﷻ
- A Cure for the hearts
- Guidance and
- Mercy for believers.

It is clear that each one of these has its own specific benefits and purpose. One should also understand that once the soul becomes connected to the physical body, it begins to enjoy the benefits of this world through the five senses, and its drowning in the joys of this world leads to corrupt beliefs and evil characteristics. The human is thus in need of a competent healer, because if such a patient does not receive a good healer, he will expire. Having understood this, we now assert that the Prophet ﷺ is that competent healer and the Quran is the collection of the four medicines which are the cures of the ills of the heart.

The four relationships between the doctor and the patient are as follows:

One: The doctor orders the patient to refrain from the things that cause the sickness. This is counsel because it forbids those things that take us away from the pleasure of Allah ﷻ and connect the heart to the *ghair ullah.*

Two: Shifā - the use of medicine to eradicate the contamination. In a similar way, the prophets would first forbid creation from engaging with dangers so that their exterior is purified of bad deeds. They then encourage intrinsic purity; the elimination of evil characteristics and the attainment of praiseworthy characteristics, all through endeavour. Thus, Shifā from evil beliefs and a vile character is the cure for the ego.

Three: Attaining Guidance - this level is achieved following the second relationship, because now the soul is ready to become the setting for Divine bounties. As Allah ﷻ is the bestower of bounties, if the heart is involved in corrupt beliefs and

10

blameworthy traits, darkness will overcome it, and whilst there is darkness, *nur* cannot enter it. When the corruption and evil disappear, the Holy light will enter into holy beings; this is the light of guidance.

Four: When the ego has attained the spiritual ranks and holy elevations mentioned above, it then attains bounties from the Solar Pearl[2] that has enlightened the whole universe. The words 'mercy for the believers' refer to this station. The believers are specified here because the souls of the disobedient do not benefit from or become enlightened by the souls of the prophets. Only the body that faces the Sun receives *nur* from the rays of the sun. If it is not facing it, the light of the Sun will not fall upon it. Similarly, until each soul has turned its attention to the court of the pure souls of the prophets, it cannot benefit from their *nur* and nor will the effects of the pure holy souls appear upon it.

In summary, this counsel signifies the purification of the exterior body. This is *Shariah*. Shifā signals the purification of the soul from corrupt beliefs and despised characteristics; this is *Tareeqat*. *Al Huda* (guidance) symbolises the appearance of the *nur* of Allah ﷻ upon the hearts of the righteous. This is *haqeeqah*. Mercy signals the perfect and spiritual level that the heart reaches, when it can become the means to perfect weak hearts. This is *nabuwwah*.

In this verse (no 57), after informing us about these divine secrets, He ﷻ then states {*Say 'with Allah's fadhl and mercy rejoice.*} The purpose of this is to inform us that these spiritual blessings are greater than the physical blessings.

In the discussion of this verse (no. 58), it is also stated that once the human individual has attained these spiritual joys, he should not be happy because of them in themselves; rather it is necessary to show happiness over the fact that they are from Allah ﷻ and this is His *fadhl*.

---

[2] Referring to the Prophet ﷺ.

11

These are the lofty and elevated secrets comprised in these words revealed from the realm of *wahi* and revelation. This is our summary of it. Some *mufassireen* have said the *fadhl* of Allah ﷻ is Islam and *rahmah* is the Quran.' *(Tafsīr Kabeer)*

Some important points

This narrative of Shaykh ul Mufassireen Imām Rāzi highlights a few important points:

1) This verse is perfect proof of the veracity of the prophethood of Muhammad.
2) Spiritual blessings are better than physical blessings.
3) Every spiritual blessing should be seen as coming from Allah ﷻ.
4) Given the previous point, one should express happiness.
5) The person of the Prophet ﷺ is the effective healer and the Quran the effective medicine.
6) This medicine will only be effective when used in accordance with the instructions of that effective healer.

An invitation to every intelligent person

After the clarification of the purpose of these verses, could any intelligent person still claim that seeing these verses as referring to the Prophet ﷺ and his arrival is contrary to the Aslāf? To take the very person these verses act to confirm out of their scope of meaning is nothing but a travesty! If it is acceptable to rejoice over the arrival of the medicine and cure (in the form of the celebration of the Quran), why is it difficult for these verses to also refer to the effective healer who brought this cure and prescription? Is this the state of our *imān*?

When this verse is able to prove the celebration of every blessing, large and small, why can it not prove joy over the one who is the source of all these blessings? If there is a command to rejoice over every *fadhl* and mercy then there must also be a command to celebrate the *Greater fadhl* and the *mercy for the Universe*.

12

Support from the other Mufassireen

One must not assume that Imām Rāzi is the only one to have mentioned this purpose of these verses; other *mufassireen* have also confirmed this purpose; take a look at a couple of the texts below.

Imām Khāzin discusses the words of this verse as:

> The meaning of the verse is that believers should rejoice at Allah's ﷻ *fadhl* and mercy, this refers to whatever Allah ﷻ bestows upon them in terms of counsel, cure of the heart, certainty of *imān* and inner contentment. {It is better than what they gather} refers to the goods of the world and its temporal joys. This is the view (of this verse) of the Ahl ul Ma'na, whereas the view of the Mufassireen is different because Ibn Abbās, Hassan and Qatāda all said that the *fadhl* of Allah ﷻ is Islam and His mercy is the Quran.
>
> *(Lubāb ut Ta'weel)*

Imām Nasafee writes about the purpose of this verse:

> Its purpose is to specify joy with *fadhl* and *rahmah* rather than with the benefits of the duniya. *(Mudārik ut Tanzeel)*

Qādhi Thanāullah Mazhari has expressed a similar view:

> Its purpose is to specify joy with the arrival of the Book or the *fadhl* and mercy and not with anything else from the fruits of this world. *(Al Mazhari)*

There is no contradiction in the meanings of the Mufassireen and the Ahl ul Haqeeqa

The Ahl ul Haqeeqa have taken it to be mean generic *fadhl* and *rahmah,* whilst the Ahl ul Tafsīr have specified two particular forms of *fadhl* and *mercy,* i.e. Islam and the Quran, thus there is no contradiction between the two.

In summary, all of these excerpts reveal that the purpose of the verse is to provide a command to express joy over spiritual benefits. Thus, it is saying: *O people, do not rejoice over the benefits of this world for they are temporary and will perish, rather rejoice over spiritual benefits which will help you in the duniya and the Ākhirah.*

Eleven Statements

One should also remember that Islam and the Quran are not the only meanings of *fadhl* and *rahmah* that the *mufassireen* mention, indeed there are 11 statements. Furthermore, Ibn Abbās also states that they mean the person of the Prophet ﷺ. Here we will go through all of these different meanings by quoting the works of Khāzin, Ruh ul Ma'āni and Mazhari:

1. Ibn Abbās, Hasan and Qatāda's view is that Allah's ﷻ *fadhl* is Islam and His mercy is the Quran.
2. It is narrated by Abu Saeed Khudri that Allah's ﷻ *fadhl* is the Quran and His mercy is the people of the Quran.
3. Ibn Umars' statement is that Allah's ﷻ *fadhl* is Islam and His mercy is the decorating of the hearts.
4. Ibn Umar also states that Allah's ﷻ *fadhl* is Islam and His mercy is *Jannah*.
5. It is also Ibn Umars that states that Allah's ﷻ *fadhl* is Islam and His mercy is the Sunnah. (Tafseer Khāzin)
6. Allāma Aloosi in Ruh ul Ma'āni also adds that Mujāhid narrated that both Allah's ﷻ *fadhl* and mercy refer to the Quran.
7. The famous Muhaddith Abu'l Shaykh states that Ibn Abbās narrated that Allah's ﷻ *fadhl* is *Ilm* (knowledge) and His mercy means the blessed person of the Prophet ﷺ.
8. Khateeb Baghdādi and Ibn Asākir narrated that Allah's ﷻ *fadhl* is the Prophet ﷺ and His mercy refers to Syeduna Ali.

After mentioning this, Allāma Aloosi writes:

Syeduna Ali is undoubtedly a mercy from Allah ﷻ for believers. But it is the Prophet ﷺ who is most famously

14

associated with the attribute of mercy, as Allah ﷻ said {*And We have not sent you but as a mercy for the Universe*} (21:107).

Have you seen how the minds of the *mufassireen* link the word *rahmah* to the Prophet ﷺ? Therefore, in what a sorry state are those who try to exclude the Prophet ﷺ from the meaning of this word!

It is clear from statements 7 and 8 that *fadhl* and *rahmah* refer to the Prophet ﷺ, and one of those who held this view was Abdullah ibn Abbās. Therefore, how can it be right to claim that none of the Aslāf took this verse to refer to the Prophet ﷺ?

9. Both of them refer to Jannah and salvation from Hell *(Ruh ul Ma'āni)*
10. Allah's ﷻ *fadhl* refers to Imān and His mercy means Jannah.
11. It is narrated by Mujāhid and Qatāda that Allah's ﷻ *fadhl* is Imān and His mercy is the Quran. *(Al Mazhari)*

There are no contradictions in these 11 statements for each one of them is referring to spiritual benefits.

Shaykh Ashraf Ali Thanvi's view

Without any disagreement, the Prophet ﷺ is Allah's ﷻ greatest blessing and His most complete *fadhl*. Thus, with scriptural evidence one can take *rahmah* and mercy to also mean the Prophet ﷺ, upon whose birth Allah ﷻ has commanded the expression of happiness.

After supporting his statement with other Quranic verses, he then states:

Although at first the prelude to this verse seems to refer to the Quran, a more general meaning, of which the Quran is an example, would be better, and in this way *fadhl* and *rahmah* can also be taken to mean the arrival of the Prophet ﷺ. With this interpretation, all blessings and mercies, whether worldly or religious, of which the Quran is one, can be included. This is because the being of the Prophet ﷺ is the source of all blessings

15

and the basis of all mercies and *fadhl*. This interpretation is the most comprehensive. On the basis of this *tafsīr,* the outcome of this verse is that it is the Lord's ﷻ proclamation that there should be happiness upon the being of the Prophet ﷺ (his *nurāni* being or his mortal birth), because he ﷺ is our means to all blessings. The best of all blessings and the greatest wealth is Imān, whose reaching us through the Prophet ﷺ is obvious.

In summary, the Prophet's ﷺ blessed person is the source of all *fadhl* and mercy. No amount of happiness over him will ever be sufficient!
(Majmua Khutbāt ba nām Milād un Nabi of Molāna Ashraf Ali Thanvi)

There is no such principle!

One must also remember that there is no such principle that states that one cannot understand the meaning of a verse in a way that the Aslāf did not. If there was such a principle, Shariah and the religion itself would become stagnant! Many events did not take place in the time of the Aslāf, so how could we use the Quran to prove rulings for them if we followed this principle?

Furthermore, was the Quranic command to reflect upon the Quran only meant for the Aslāf? No intelligent person could ever claim this! To the people of knowledge, the command to reflect upon the Quran applies until the coming of Qiyāmah. If it was compulsory to only use the Aslāf's interpretation, what would be the purpose of the command to reflect? Imām Qurtubi mentions this claim before rejecting it with evidence:

Some of the ulema state that the tafsīr must be based upon precedent *(simaa)* because of Allah's ﷻ statement *{Then if you disagree in anything, refer it to Allah and the Messenger} (4:59).* This claim is wrong. Do we know what type of tafsīr the Quran forbids? Does it mean that we imitate and follow and forsake inference, or does it mean something else? To believe it means that tafsīr is restricted to *simā* is wrong, because even the Sahāba disagreed over tafsīr, and after all, was all that they

16

related based entirely on the statement of the Prophet ﷺ? Furthermore, the Prophet ﷺ supplicated for Ibn Abbās, 'O Allah, give him insight into the dīn and knowledge of interpreting the Quran'. If, like the Quran, the tāwīl and tafsīr were restricted to *simā,* why make this dua for him? This (matter) is perfectly clear and there is no difficulty in it.

(Al Jāme Li Ahkām il Quran)

Instead the principle is...

The principle is that any (other) tafsīr that contradicts the tafsīr mentioned by the Aslāf is rejected. Shaykh Muhammad bin Musli writes:

> To mention a statement in the tafsīr of Allah's ﷻ Book that is against the tafsīr of the salaf and Imāms necessitates one of two things; either the new statement is wrong or the statement of the salaf is wrong. Every intelligent person will deem the new statement wrong because it is better to call it wrong than calling the statement of the salaf wrong. *(al Qowl ul Fasal)*

Firstly, it has already been made clear that the *mufassir* of the Quran Abdullah bin Abbās took *rahmah* to mean the person of the Prophet ﷺ. Furthermore, even if this had not been everyone's statement, there is no harm in taking it to mean the Prophet ﷺ because it does not contradict the tafsīr of the Aslāf in any way. How can those who take this verse to only mean the Quran and Islam exclude the man of the Quran and Islam from it? Shaykh Ibn Qayyim, for example, takes it to mean Islam and the Sunnah, and the proof he provides is how one attains happiness from them:

> In accordance with the condition of the heart, there will be happiness over Islam and the Sunnah. As this acquaintance increases, so too will happiness. The person acting upon the Sunnah has a living and enlightened heart whilst the one in Bid'ah has a dead and dark heart. *(al Qowl ul Fasal)*

17

If happiness and joy are attained through acting upon the Sunnah of the blessed person, there should be greater joy and happiness from the remembrance of that blessed person! Indeed, belief in Islam and Sunnah come later; it is first necessary to believe in that blessed person for one's Islam and Sunnah cannot be reliable without belief in him!

The wisdom in the word Qul (say)

It is for this reason that Allah ﷻ started this statement with 'Qul' (meaning 'Say'); so that the ummah remember that both Islam and the Quran are because of and through the Prophet ﷺ. As soon as one remembers any of Allah's ﷻ blessings, *fadhl* and kindness, one should immediately acknowledge that these were attained through and because of the Prophet ﷺ.

Thus, where there is a command to rejoice over Islam and the Quran, there must undoubtedly be the command to rejoice over its means and cause! Allah ﷻ knew that there would be some who would include the Quran, Sunnah and Islam in this verse but exclude the Prophet ﷺ; thus He began the verse with 'Qul' so that from the very first word, one's attention is drawn to the Prophet ﷺ.

When will it contradict the Aslāf?

At the end of this discussion, one should be certain of when a tafsīr contradicts the Aslāf; it is when one claims that the verse commands the rejoicing of worldly benefits. However, no one suggests such a thing. The Mawlid gathering is simply the remembrance of Allah ﷻ and His Prophet ﷺ, which are a source of spiritual benefits.

18

Mawlid and the Sunnah of the Prophet ﷺ

Here we will recall just three acts of the Prophet ﷺ in commemoration of the Mawlid, which our Aslāf (elders) have taken as proof of the permissibility of the Mawlid gathering.

1. The Fast of Monday

The Prophet ﷺ would fast every Monday. Syeduna Qatāda asked him about this practice and he ﷺ replied:

> This is the day upon which I was born and on which it (Quran) was revealed. *(Muslim, Book of Siyām)*

Using this hadith as evidence of the Mawlid gathering, Shaykh Muhammad Alawi al Māliki writes that it is clear that through this blessed act,

> He ﷺ (highlights) the greatness of the day of his birth; and expressed gratitude to Allah ﷻ for His greatest blessing upon him on that day and for his existence, because it brought good fortune to all of creation. All this was expressed through fasting, and this too is what the Mawlid gathering is about; even if its form differs, its purpose is the same, whether it be fasting, distributing food, gathering for the Dhikr and Salawāt upon the Prophet ﷺ, or listening to his ﷺ honoured *Shamāil* (characteristics).
>
> *(Muqaddima Mawrid arRawā 9-10)*

In other words, the underlying basis of all of these acts is the same; to thank Allah ﷻ for His greatest blessing.

19

Shaykh Ibn Rajab Hanbali (d795h) writes that this hadith proves it is *mustahab* to fast on the days in which a blessing of Allah ﷻ is received, and the greatest blessing for the Ummah was the arrival of the Prophet ﷺ!

> In it (this hadith) is a signal of the fact that it is good practice to fast on the days in which Allah ﷻ bestows His servants with a blessing. And surely the greatest blessing upon this Ummah is the appearance of Muhammad ﷺ, his mission and his prophethood, just as Allah ﷻ says, {Undoubtedly, Allah favoured the believers when He sent to them the Messenger}. Undoubtedly, the sending of the Prophet ﷺ is a blessing greater than the blessings of the Sky, Earth, Sun, Moon, Wind, Night, Day, Rain, vegetation etc. Of course, these (latter mentioned) blessings are great blessings for all humanity, even for those who have rejected Allah ﷻ and His Prophet ﷺ and show ingratitude. But with the arrival of the Prophet ﷺ, all the virtues of this and the next world were perfected. Because of him the religion was completed just as Allah ﷻ had wished it to be for His servants, and whose acceptance would lead to prosperity in this and the next world. Consequently, fasting on the days these blessings were received from Allah ﷻ is a beautiful deed, and this is a part of renewing one's gratitude for the blessing. The day of Ashura is an example of this.   *(Latāif ul Mu'ārif 189)*

2. Sacrificing an animal in gratitude in Madīnah

Imām Suyooti writes that he believes that evidence for the Mawlid in the ahadith is the Prophet's ﷺ act in Madīnah of sacrificing an animal in commemoration of his birth and in gratitude to Allah ﷻ. Some have claimed this act to be *aqeeqah*[3], but Imām Suyooti rejects this by explaining that the *aqeeqah* of the Prophet ﷺ had been performed by the Prophet's ﷺ grandfather Abd'ul Muttalib:

> The aqeeqah is not repeated again, so this act of the Prophet ﷺ has to be interpreted as a display of gratitude to Allah ﷻ for

---

[3] Sacrifice offered at the birth of a child, usually on the 7th day.

20

making him the *Rahmat ulil Ālameen* (mercy for the Universe) and to make it permissible for his Ummah.

(Husn ul Maqsid fi Amal il Mawlid 196)

3. The Fast of Ashura

Bukhāri and Muslim narrate from Abdullah ibn Abbās that when the Prophet ﷺ arrived in Madīnah,

> He ﷺ found the Jews fasting on the day of Ashura and enquired from them about it. They replied, 'This is the day on which Allah gave victory to Musa and the Bani Israil over Firawn and we fast in its (the day's) honour'.
>
> *(Bukhāri & Muslim)*

To this, the Prophet ﷺ replied:

> 'We are closer to Musa than you' and ordered the fast.
>
> *(Bukhāri)*

In a second narration by Bukhāri, the Prophet ﷺ ordered the companions,

> You have more right to Musa than them so fast on it.

When the Imām ul Muhadditheen Hāfiz Ibn Hajar was asked about the gathering of Mawlid, in terms of its permissibility, he referred to this hadith and said:

> The narration of the Sahihain (Bukhāri and Muslim) holds the rank of sanad (precedent) in the permissibility of the gathering of Mawlid. *(Al Mawrid Ar Rawā 31)*

Consequently, if it is permissible to commemorate the day upon which Allah ﷻ favoured Musa ﷺ and his ummah, how can it be a bid'ah and deviation to show gratitude when Allah ﷻ blessed this ummah with the greatest favour, about which even Musa ﷺ said in envy, 'O

Allah, make me from his Ummah'[4]. Not only that, but as the Prophet ﷺ is the greatest blessing, it is more important for this Ummah to show gratitude. Hāfiz Ibn Hajar explained this in the following:

It is apparent from this prophetic act that Allah ﷻ should be thanked on the day on which His blessing is received or a catastrophe is lifted, and He should also be thanked when that day returns. There are many ways of thanking Allah ﷻ; worship, prostration, fasting, charity and recitation.

(Al Mawrid Ar Rawā 31)

After this prelude, he turns the reader's attention to the fact that all blessings have their respective places but,

The greatest blessing of all is the arrival of the honourable Prophet ﷺ on that day.　　　　　*(Al Mawrid Ar Rawā 31)*

Imitating Christmas?

An oft-quoted objection is, 'the celebration of Mawlid is similar to (or an imitation of) the act of the Christians who celebrate the day of the birth of Isa'. To this we respond in the following way:

---

[4] Allāh ﷻ ordered Musa عليه السلام to inform the Bani Israil: 'Whoever meets Me as a rejector of Ahmad I will put him into Hell, no matter who he may be.' Musa عليه السلام asked who Ahmad was and was informed, 'O Musa, I swear by My Honour and Majesty I have not created anything more respected to me than him. I wrote his name next to mine on the Arsh two million years before creating the Heavens, Earth, Sun and Moon. I swear by My Honour and Majesty that Jannah is forbidden for all of creation until I have sent Muhammad and his Ummah into it.' (Then in the fadāil of the Ummah it is that) Musa عليه السلام pleaded, 'O Lord, make me a prophet of that nation.' Allāh ﷻ explained, 'Its prophet will come from it.' He then pleaded, 'Make me from that Ummah (a follower of Muhammad).' He was told, 'You are before and he will come after, however I will join you and him in the *Dār ul Jalāl* (Jannah)'. This is narrated in Hilya.

The above-mentioned hadith should extinguish such an objection because no one knows the Shariah better than the legislator himself! Furthermore, according to (this logic of) the critics, the Prophet ﷺ should have prohibited fasting on the day of Ashura because the Jews were already fasting on that day. However, rather than forbidding such similarly in good acts, he ﷺ ordered a show of greater love and directed the companions to fast as well. So what room is there for such an objection?

Remember that the similarities with unbelievers that Islam forbids are in terms of beliefs and acts that contradict Islam. It is mandatory to refrain from such things for Allah ﷻ will be displeased with anyone who undertakes them.

It is for this reason that those party to the inner secrets of Islam have actually claimed that if Christians celebrate the day of their saviour's birth, Muslims should celebrate the day of their prophet's birth with even greater fervour! Far from being an imitation of unbelievers, this would in fact be the living death of satanic forces. Look at what Imām ul Qurā Hafiz ul Hadith Shaykh Ibn Jazari writes:

In it (Mawlid) is death for satanic forces and life for believers. So when Christians take the day of the birth of their prophet [saviour] as their greatest Eid, Muslims have a greater responsibility to honour the Mawlid of their prophet.

(Al Mawrid Ar Rawā 29-30)

Why Every Year?

It is also sometimes said that 'the birth of the Prophet ﷺ happened once and that day has passed. This event does not happen each year so what is the need to commemorate it (each year)?' The simple response is this:

The Prophet's ﷺ own act above bears witness to the fact that when the day on which a specific bounty of Allah ﷻ occurred returns, it is commemorated with gratitude. When the Jews revealed that this was the day on which Allah ﷻ gave salvation to Musa السلام and the Bani Israil, and destroyed Firawn and his nation, the Prophet ﷺ declared that in future, he would also fast and ordered the companions to do so as well. If it was wrong to commemorate that day each year,

23

who would be more aware of that than the Prophet ﷺ himself? Rather than forbidding it, he ﷺ established the principle that the day on which a blessing of Allah ﷻ occurred should be remembered through a show of happiness.

In using this hadith as a reference, Shaykh Muhammad Alawi Māliki states:

> The Prophet ﷺ took account of those times in which religious events took place and when those times returned, he would honour them by showing happiness in remembrance of the religious event. (This is) because that day became the 'arena' for that religious matter. The Prophet ﷺ blessed us with this principle himself through his actions and words; for example the authentic hadith in which he ﷺ saw the Jews in Madīnah fasting on Ashura and ordered the companions to fast as well.
> *(Muqaddima Al Mawrid Ar Rawā 10)*

Furthermore, all of the days that are celebrated in Islam are in reality in remembrance (of something). Take for example the celebration of the Quran's revelation, it is celebrated each year yet the Quran is not revealed anew each year. Similarly, Jumu'ah is in remembrance of Syeduna Adam ﷺ, whilst other days include the fast of Ashura, the Night of Qadr and the Night of Barā'a! So when each of these days returns with all its blessings, how great will be the remembrance of the day of the Prophet's ﷺ birth?

Proof of the Mawlid gathering from the narration of Abbās

Syeduna Abbās narrates that he saw Abu Lahab in a dream a year after he died. He was in a very bad state, complaining,

> I have had no respite since separating from you, save that the punishment is reduced each Monday.

For what reason was his punishment reduced? Understand this from Syeduna Abbās' own words:

24

Verily the Prophet ﷺ was born on a Monday. Abu Lahab's slave girl Thowbiya gave this good news to him and in happiness he freed her. Consequently, every Monday, Allah ﷻ reduces his punishment.

(Fath ul Bāri Shar ul Bukhāri 9:145)

The Ulema deduce from this that if even an unbeliever is rewarded for celebrating the birth of the Prophet ﷺ, how could a Muslim be deprived (of reward if he celebrates the Prophet's ﷺ birth)? Look at the statements of the elders of the critics themselves on this matter:

The son of Muhammad bin Abdul Wahhāb Najdi writes, with reference to Ibn Jowzi:

If this is the state of the unbeliever Abu Lahab, in whose condemnation a chapter of the Quran was revealed, and he is rewarded for being happy on the night of the Prophet's ﷺ Mawlid, what will be the state of the Muwahhid Muslim who celebrates his Mawlid?

(Muktathar Sīra tur Rasool 13)

Mufti Rashid Ahmad Ludhiyānvi writes:

If the punishment of an unbeliever such as Abu Lahab is reduced because he celebrated the birth of the Prophet ﷺ, how can any one of the Prophet's ﷺ Ummah who out of love celebrates his birth and spends to his ability fail to attain the elevated ranks?!

(Ahsan ul Fatāwa 1:347)

The gathering of the Companions

The Companions would always mention this great blessing and show gratitude to Allah ﷻ for it.

Syeduna Muāwiya narrates that one day the Prophet ﷺ came out of his blessed room and saw the Companions seated and asked, 'What are you seated for?' They replied:

25

'We are gathered to remember Allah ﷻ and praise Him for gifting us with His dīn and favouring us with you.'
On hearing these words he ﷺ said,
'Verily Allah ﷻ is taking pride in your act with the Angels.'

Abdullah bin Abbās narrates that the Companions were once gathered and were discussing the ranks and splendours of the different prophets; one said that Adam was Safi ullah, another that Musa was Kaleem ullah, a third that Isa was Ruh ullah, whilst another said Ibraheem was Khalil ullah. During this the Prophet ﷺ arrived and said:

What you have said I have heard and it is all true but listen, I am Habeeb ullah (Allah's beloved), yet I take no pride in it.
(Mishkāt ul Masābeeh)

Look carefully; if this is not a Mawlid gathering then what is it? If such a gathering was impermissible, the Prophet ﷺ would have forbidden it, however, instead he states the virtues of such gatherings by saying that Allah ﷻ takes pride in them. Furthermore, by becoming part of these gatherings, he also revealed their status.

As the Quran and Sunnah contain the command to express happiness over the Prophet's ﷺ arrival, it is therefore permissible to express this happiness - whilst always staying within the limits of Shariah - according to the ways and customs of the time and place, for example, processions, lamps etc. There is evidence of this in the ahadith; at the time of his birth did the stars not draw near his house? The mother of Abu'l Ās states:

I was present at the time of the Prophet's ﷺ birth and I saw his house become covered in *nur*. The stars were so close that I feared they would fall on me.   *(Bayhaqi and Tibrāni)*

Did the angels at the time of his birth not plant flags in the East and the West and upon the roof of the Ka'bah? Did the angels, prophets and *hoors* not travel in a procession to Syeda Āminah's house to congratulate her? If one finds it difficult to read about these events, one should at least read the books of sīra and the spectacle presented by the people of Madīnah when welcoming the Prophet ﷺ into their city! Was that not an expression of happiness? Was that not a procession? Were candles and lamps not lit? Were there no flags flying? Were songs of happiness not sung collectively? Were chants confirming his prophethood not raised? Were the walls of the city not resonating with the calls of *Yā Muhammad* and *Yā Rasoolallah*?!

If there is proof of all these things – and undoubtedly there is – how have these things now become bid'ah and illegal after they were once undertaken by the legislator of Shariah himself ﷺ?! If, after all this, people still want proof from the first generation then one can only feel sorry for them!

One other objection sometimes raised is that the Quran and Sunnah discuss the *baitha* (revelation of his prophethood) and not his ﷺ birth, thus one should commemorate the *baitha* and not the birth. Our viewpoint is that both are Allah's ﷺ blessings and one should rejoice in both; however the birth is the means to the *baitha*. If there had been no birth, how would there have been *baitha*? As for the issue of whether the birth is or is not mentioned in the scriptures, we will present some verses and ahadith and let the reader decide.

The Quran and his transfer into pure loins

In Sura Shu'ara Allah ﷺ addresses His beloved in the following way:

> And put your trust in the Almighty, Ever-Merciful (Lord), Who sees you when you stand up (for Tahajjud Prayer in the solitary hours of the night). And Who (also keeps) seeing your transferring amongst those who prostrate themselves in Prayer. Verily, He is All-Hearing, All-Knowing.'
>
> *(Quran 26: 217-220)*

The interpreter of the Quran, Syeduna Abdullah bin Abbās, mentions the tafsīr of this verse as:

> 'Transferring' refers to the move from the pure loins of his forefathers up until He ﷺ made you a prophet.
>
> *(Masālim ul Hunafā)*

27

It is written in Tafsīr Jaml that Allah ﷻ oversaw all the loins and wombs the Prophet ﷺ passed through from Syeduna Adam and Syeda Hawa ﵇ to Syeduna Abdullah and Syeda Āminah:

> O beloved, your Lord is overseeing all the believing loins and wombs you passed through from Syeduna Adam and Hawa ﵇ to Syeduna Abdullah and Āminah. Thus all your ancestors – male and female – are believers.

Consider the words of Sāwi alal Jalālayn:

> It means that He ﷻ saw you transferring from the loins and wombs of believers, from Adam ﵇ to Abdullah.

Look at how the Quran describes his transference between the different loins and wombs, all of which were before his birth. Now let us inspect the account of his birth.

The Quran and the oath of the begotten

The Quran recalls his birth by taking an oath upon his being born:

> (O My Esteemed Beloved!) By (your) father (Adam or Ibrahim [Abraham]) and by the begotten.'   *(Quran 90:3)*

In this verse Allah ﷻ has taken the oath of two honourable personalities; the father and the begotten. 'Father' refers to every father through whom the *nur* of Muhammad passed until it reached Syeduna Abdullah, after which it appeared in the human form from the blessed womb of Syeda Āminah. The verse then takes the oath of the begotten, for whose birth this whole universe was brought into being.

Qādi Thanā ullah Pāni Patti writes below this verse:

> 'The *father*' refers to Adam or Ibrahim ﵇ or to every father whilst 'the *begotten*' refers to Muhammad ﷺ.
>
> *(Mazhari)*

28

Allāma Jār ullah Zamakshari explains this in the form of a question and answer:

> And if you were to ask the meaning of 'By the father and the begotten', I would say the Prophet ﷺ and from whom he was begotten. First, Allah ﷻ took the oath of his ﷺ (the Prophet's) city, which was his place of birth and the haram (sanctity) of his father Ibraheem and Ismail ﷺ. He then took the oath of every person who became his ﷺ [the Prophet's] father, and then finally took an oath by the Prophet ﷺ himself.
>
> *(Al kashāf)*

Imām Nizām ud dīn Hassan Muhammad Neshapuri states the view of the majority of the *mufassireen* in these words:

> And most of them are of the view that the father refers to Ibraheem and Ismaeel ﷺ, and the begotten [refers to] Muhammad ﷺ. He ﷺ first took the oath of his city, then his father and then his.
>
> *(Garāib ul Quran)*

Allāma Baidāwi writes:

> The father is Adam or Ibraheem ﷺ and the begotten is their offspring or the Prophet Muhammad ﷺ.

This verse mentions his birth in an extremely beautiful way; the form of an oath. Following this, the Quran also mentions his childhood.

The Quran and the Prophet's ﷺ childhood

Sura Ad Duhā, as well as recalling the Divine favours upon the Prophet ﷺ and his lofty station, also mentions the following favour:

> (O Beloved!) Did He not find you an orphan, and then provide you (with a dignifying and graceful) abode?   *(Quran 93:6)*

The Prophet ﷺ did not become an orphan after his *baitha* but was so from birth! By mentioning his orphanhood and the Divine favours upon him, is Allah ﷻ not mentioning the conditions of his childhood? Now let us look at the Quranic verses about his life before his *baitha*.

His life before baitha: the greatest proof of Tawheed

The Quran reveals that the first piece of evidence for *tawheed*, prophethood and Islam that the Prophet ﷺ presented was his own blessed life before his *baitha*. Allah ﷻ reveals that His beloved said:

> I have indeed spent a (part of) life amongst you (even) before this (revelation of the Qur'an). So do you not understand?'
> *(Quran 10: 16)*

In other words, the Prophet ﷺ is saying that despite living in this society of *jahiliyya,* he had never lied on any occasion, so how could he suddenly speak falsely about the Tawheed of Allah ﷻ?

Ponder how the Quran presents all the events of his childhood and youth as proof of the veracity of Islam, and yet some of his followers now claim that the Quran only mentions his *baitha* and nothing of the Prophet's ﷺ life before it! One can only feel sorrow over this state of affairs!

Allah ﷻ took an oath on his whole life!

Now let us look at that verse of the Quran where Allah ﷻ took an oath on his ﷺ whole life, both before his *baitha* and after it. He said:

> By your life, [O Muhammad], indeed they were, in their intoxication, wandering blindly.   *(Quran 15:72)*

Now is there any part of his ﷺ life, from his birth to his passing which is not within the scope of this verse? Thus, it is nothing but slander to claim that the Quran only mentions the *baitha* and not his birth; such a claim does not befit a Muslim.

30

He was born on the 12th of Rabi Ul Awwal

As for the claim that it is not proven that he ﷺ was born on the 12th of Rabi ul Awwal, there is definitely a difference of opinion amongst the ulema, but the view of the majority is that his ﷺ birth was on the 12th of Rabi ul Awwal.

Here we will mention some statements of the Companions, Tābi'een, great Mufassireen, Muhadditheen and historians who assert that the 12th of Rabi ul Awwal is his ﷺ date of birth.

The Statements of Syeduna Jābir and Ibn Abbās

Hāfiz Abu Bakr bin Abi Shayba, d.235 hijri, narrates the following sahih about the Prophet's ﷺ birth:

> It was Jābir and Ibn Abbās who both said that the Prophet ﷺ was born in the Year of the Elephant on Monday, the 12th of Rabi ul Awwal.
>
> *(Musannaf Ibn Abi Shayba)*

The Statement of Imām Muhammad bin Isāc Tābi'ee

Imām Muhammad bin Isāc Tābi'ee was the first sīra chronicler of the Islamic world and wrote the following about the blessed birth:

> The Prophet ﷺ was born on a Monday, the 12th night of the month of Rabi ul Awwal in the Year of the Elephant.

Hafiz Ibn Katheer, d.774 hijri, cites the narration of Syeduna Jābir and Syeduna Ibn Abbās that the Prophet's ﷺ birth was on the 12th of Rabi ul Awwal of the Year of the Elephant, and then declares:

> This is the most famous statement according to the majority.
>
> *(As Sīra tun Nabawiyya)*

Ibn Sayyid un Nās writes:

> Our Master and Prophet Muhammad ﷺ, the messenger of Allah, was born on the 12th night of the month of Rabi ul Awwal in the Year of the Elephant. *(Uyoon ul Athār)*

Shaykh Abdul Haque ad Dehlvi, in making a judgement on this matter, states:

> There is disagreement over this; some believe it is the 12th of Rabi ul Awwal, others believe it is the 2nd, while a number state it is the 8th. The statement of the 12th is the majority [view] and is the most famous. The practice of the people of Makkah also testifies this date because it is on this night that they visit the Prophet's ﷺ place of birth and hold a Mawlid gathering.
> *(Mudārij an Nabuwwah)*

The renowned scholar of Egypt, Shaykh Muhammad Abu Zahra, writes that this is the view of all the great people of *rivāyah* (narration):

> All the great scholars of hadith and history agree that his birth took place in Rabi ul Awwal of the Year of the Elephant, on the 12th night.
> *(Khātim un Nabiyyeen)*

The view of Mufti Muhammad Shafee Deobandi

There is agreement over the fact that the virtuous birth took place on a Monday in the month of Rabi ul Awwal, but there are four different statements regarding the date. The most famous statement concerns the 12th; to such an extent that Ibn Bazzār declared ijma upon it, and it is what Kāmil Ibn Atheer also preferred.

Further on in rejecting the views of the others, Mufti Shafee writes:

> The date of the 9th, which Mahmud Pāsha al Misri preferred in light of his calculation, is against the majority view and is an

32

unsubstantiated statement. Furthermore, a calculation is not so reliable that one can go against the majority because of it.

(Sira Khātim ul Ambiya)

Thus, from the time of the sahāba to this very day, every person of knowledge believes that the blessed birth took place on the 12th of Rabi ul Awwal, so to claim otherwise is an act of great boldness.

He passed away on this day?

It is often said that the 12th of Rabi ul Awwal was the date of the Prophet's ﷺ passing and so it is wholly inappropriate to celebrate and hold gatherings on such a sad day.

However, there is disagreement over the date of his ﷺ passing. We present the view of Allāma Shibli, who concludes at the end of his three pages on this topic:

It is for this reason that near us the authentic date of the Prophet's ﷺ death is the first of Rabi ul Awwal.

(Hāshiya Sīra tun Nabi)

Even if the 12th was the Prophet's ﷺ date of passing, there is still no scope for objection, for both the Quran and Sunnah make clear that the Prophet's ﷺ birth and his passing are a source of good for the Ummah. Syeduna Abdullah ibn Masood narrates the Prophet's ﷺ statement:

My life is good for you all and my death is good for you.

(As Shifā 1:19)

On another occasion, whilst explaining that death can be a good thing, the Prophet ﷺ said:

When Allah ﷻ intends to bestow His specific kindness and favour upon a nation, He ﷻ brings death to the prophet of that nation and makes him an intercessor and forbearer for them; and when He intends the destruction of a nation, He ﷻ punishes and destroys it during the earthly lifetime of that nation's prophet, and through this destruction, He ﷻ cools the eyes of that prophet. *(Muslim 2:249)*

Mulla Ali Qāri explains the term 'forbearer' in this hadith as:

Forbearer refers to the person who precedes others to a destination and furnishes it with provisions for those who follow. It is used to describe the one who intercedes for those who follow. *(As Shifā)*

What a great blessing and favour Allah ﷻ has bestowed upon this nation by making the Prophet ﷺ its intercessor for the Hereafter. This is why the Prophet ﷺ explained that his passing away was a mercy for the Ummah.

The birth is the greatest blessing

As the above Prophetic statement clearly demonstrates, both the birth and passing of the Prophet ﷺ are blessings for the ummah, so the next question is which is the greater blessing? It seems obvious that the birth is the greater blessing for the second blessing – his passing – could not have happened but for the first.

Imām Jalāluddin Suyooti makes an excellent point that Islam orders its adherents to express happiness on the occasion of the Prophet's ﷺ birth by way of the Aqeeqah etc., but does not order anything on the occasion of the Prophet's ﷺ death, in fact, it forbids lamentation and wailing.

Shar'ī principles teach that in the month of Rabi ul Awwal, happiness at the Prophet's ﷺ birth should be expressed and not sadness at his passing away.
(Al Hāwi lil Fatāwa)

Mufti Inayat Ahmad Kākorvi writes the following about the people of the Haramain:

The Ulema have written that the Prophet's ﷺ death should not be mentioned in this gathering because this gathering is intended to express the happiness of the Mawlid and so mentioning sadness does not befit the gathering. It is certainly not the practice of the Haramain to mention the events of his passing. *(Tawārīkh Habeeb e Ilāhi)*

We should realise that we would only mourn the passing of the Prophet ﷺ if his blessings had come to an end. However, this is not the case, Praise be to Allah ﷻ, they will continue until Qi yāmah and beyond! Even today, we are still living in his era of prophethood and the entire Ummah is based upon his ﷺ mercy and kindness. In other words, his passing did not end his relationship with the Ummah for his ﷺ blessings continue today and his life now is greater than his earthly life. The fault lies with us for he ﷺ hears and sees today just as he ﷺ heard and saw during his earthly life.

The teacher of the Muhadditheen, Mulla Ali Qāri, describes his passing away so brilliantly:

Here it is neither death nor passing but moving from one state to another. *(Shara Shifā 1:36)*

You will have noticed that our Imāms have been clear that this is not death but simply a change or transfer, so where there is no death, why should there be mourning?

Oppressive Ruler?

Some object that the ruler of the time was oppressive and the scholar who wrote about the Mawlid was a liar[5]. The first point to bear in mind is that, as the Mawlid gathering has been proven by the Quran and

---

[5] Some have said that the ruler of Irbil, who would hold a large Mawlid gathering, was an oppressive and unjust ruler and thus his practice of Mawlid was incorrect. Similarly the great scholar of the time, Shaykh bin Dahiyā, who wrote a book on the topic of the Mawlid, is also unjustly condemned by some today. See 'The Birth of the Prophet ﷺ' by Justice Shaykh Karam Shah Al Azhari for further accounts of the Mawlid gathering organised by this ruler.

Ahadith, there is no need to look further. Secondly, is the critics' opinion on these two individuals agreed upon by all of the ulema? If not, honesty dictates that both views should be presented to allow people to decide for themselves in light of the full facts. If one was to read Imām Jalāl ud dīn Suyooti's *'Husn al maqsid fil amal il Mowlid'*, the matter would become clear. We will present the view of three universally-accepted elders, after which, the reader can make up their own mind.

Hafiz Ibn Katheer's states that he was a great, generous leader and king and all his actions were very good:

> The King Muzaffar Abu Saeed organised a blessed Mawlid in the month of Rabi ul Awwal. He was a very courageous, wise and just ruler. May Allah ﷻ have mercy on him.
>
> *(Al Hāwi lil Fatāwa)*

Imām Jalāl ud dīn Suyooti in Husn ul Maqsid writes:

> The ruler of Irbil, the Mālik al Muzaffar Abu Saeed, was one of the grand, great kings who left a positive legacy.

In *mira' tu zamān,* the grandson of Ibn Jowzi writes that along with spending a great amount on the Mawlid, the King would spend 100,000 dinār on hospitality for the guests, and people from every sphere of society would be present.

> Similarly, he would give 200,000 dinār to the Europeans in return for the freedom of 60,000 captive Muslims. He would also spend 30,000 dinār a year on the maintenance of the haramain and providing water to the pilgrims. These charities were in addition to those he gave discretely. His wife, Lady Rabee'a bint Ayub (who was the sister of Sultan Nāsir Salāhuddīn), would say that her husband's shirt was made from heavy coarse cotton, costing no more than 5 dirhams. She once mentioned this to him and he replied that wearing a five-dirham shirt and giving the rest of his money in sadaqah was much more important to him than wearing an expensive shirt and not

being able to help the poor and destitute.

(Al Hāwi lil Fatāwa)

He also ordered that, upon his death, he be buried in the blessed haram.

After all this, if anyone still insists on labelling such a ruler as 'pleasure-seeking' or oppressive, he should fear his own grave and wait for the day when all truths will become evident. As for Shaykh Al Hāfiz Abu'l Khitāb bin Dahiyā[6], he too is universally-accepted. Ibn Khalqān writes the following about him:

He was of the great ulema and famous fudala.

(Al Hāwi lil Fatāwa)

If he wrote a book on the Prophet's ﷺ Mawlid and the ruler of the time rewarded him with 1,000 dinār, what is wrong with that? The Prophet's ﷺ Creator and Ruler rewarded unbelievers such as Abu Lahab for displaying happiness at his birth. Is a reduction in Allah's ﷻ punishment the same as 1,000 dinār? Surely nothing compares to Allah's ﷻ reward! If that ruler simply followed this divine Sunnah, why issue a fatwa against him?

Furthermore, these individuals were not the only ones to organise a Mawlid gathering or provide material for them. One could fill an entire book with the names of all those who have written on this issue. Some of the ulema and their writings are mentioned in the next chapter. A brief listing is included at Appendix 2.

---

[6] The scholar who wrote a book on the Mawlid during the time of the King of Irbil.

The views of some Great Ulema on the Mawlid

Throughout history, scholars have had only praise for the Mawlid gatherings. Only recently have a minority of people, for some reason, begun to object to the Mawlid. Such people should ask themselves whether they know Islam better than the great scholars listed below.

The Muhaddith Ibn Jowzi

From the first of Rabi ul Awwal, the people of the honourable Haramain; Egypt; Yemen; Syria and all the other Arab cities in the East and West celebrate the gathering of Mawlid an Nabawi. The main events (in them) are the recitation of and listening to the (events of) Mawlid. Through these (gatherings), people attain great reward and many spiritual successes.

(Al Mīlād un Nabi, 58)

Imām Abu Shāma, the Shaykh of Imām Nawawi

Among the excellent new acts started in our time in the city of Irbil is the giving of sadaqah and display of splendour and happiness on the anniversary of Mawlid an Nabawi. (This is an excellent act) because alongside supporting the poor, it also reveals the love, greatness and respect for the Prophet ﷺ (that exists) in our hearts and our gratitude to Allah ﷻ for sending His Prophet ﷺ as a Mercy for all the Worlds.

(Al Bāith Alā Inkār ul Bid'a wal Hawādith p13)

Imām Al Hāfiz Sakhāwi

In all the great cities, Muslims celebrate in the nights in the month of the Mawlid with great gatherings, increased Sadaqah, and good deeds. The events at the time of the Prophet's ﷺ birth in particular are the subject of these gatherings.

(Subl ul Hudā 1:439)

Imām Jalāludin Suyooti

I believe that the acts of the Mawlid; the gathering of people, the recitation of the Quran, the narration of the Prophet's ﷺ sīra and the signs that appeared at the time of his birth are *bid'ah hasana* (a beautiful innovation) worthy of reward, for they are undertaken to reveal respect and love for the Prophet ﷺ and express happiness at his arrival.

(Husn ul Maqsid Fi Amal il Mawlid Fi'l Hāwi li'l Fatāwa1:189)

Imām Qustalāni, the commentator of Bukhāri

Muslims have always been celebrating through gatherings in Rabi ul Awwal, the month of his [the Prophet's ﷺ] birth. In these nights, they increase Sadaqah and good deeds; in particular, they attain Allah's ﷻ mercy by narrating the Prophet's ﷺ birth in these gatherings. The gathering of Mawlid is proven to bring barakah, which ensures peace throughout the year. May Allah ﷻ shower his favour and bounty upon the one who celebrates the Mawlid as an Eid and (in doing so casts) affliction upon the one with sickness (of opposition) in his heart.

(Al Muwāhib ul ludduniya 1:27)

Shaykh Ibn Taymiyya

The motive of those who celebrate the Mawlid is either to imitate the Christians who celebrate the birth of Isa ﷺ, or their

39

motivation is solely the love and respect of the Prophet ﷺ. If it is for the latter purpose then Allah ﷻ will reward them (for this love and effort).

(Iqtidā Sirāt al Mustaqeem, 294)

In another place he wrote:

If the purpose of the Mawlid gathering is respect for the Prophet ﷺ then there is great reward for [those who celebrate it], as I have stated before.

(Iqtidā Sirāt al Mustaqeem, 297)

There is no other reason for a person to perform Mawlid but out of respect and love for the Prophet ﷺ.

Hāfiz Abu Zar'a Al Irāqi

It was asked if the Mawlid practice was Mustahab or Makruh and if any scripture existed which could be used as guidance (in this matter). He replied:

Distributing food is Mustahab at all times so think how great it will be when it is combined with the happiness of the appearance of the Prophet's ﷺ nur in the month of Rabi ul Awwal. We do not know if the Aslāf did this, but just because it was not done before does not make it Bid'ah or Makruh. Indeed, there are many good acts which were not in the Aslāf, and some of them are Wājib!

(Tathneef ul Ādhān of Shaykh Muhammad bin Siddiq p136)

Imām Ibn Hajar Makki

Most of the gatherings of Mawlid and Dhikr that take place around us are based on virtue because they contain Sadaqah, Dhikr and Salawāt and Salām upon the Prophet ﷺ.

(Fatāwa Hadithiya p129)

40

Mulla Ali Qāri

The Shuyookh and Ulema of all countries respect the gathering of Mawlid such that not one of them refuses to participate in them. The reason for their participation is the attainment of barakah.

(Al Mawrid ar Rawā)

Imām Naseeruddin (better known as BāBin Tabākh)

When a man on the night of Mawlid gives sadaqah and organises authentic narrations that become reminders of Ākhirah, all with joy at the birth of the Prophet ﷺ, there is no doubt of its permissibility. There is reward for the one who does this with such good intentions.

(Subl ul Hudā 1:144)

Imām Jamāl uddin Al Katāni

The day of the Prophet's ﷺ birth is extremely honoured, holy and respected. The Prophet ﷺ is salvation for the one who follows him. Whoever expresses happiness at his arrival protects himself from the punishments of Hell. Consequently, expressing happiness on these occasions and spending as much as one can afford is highly appropriate.

(Subl ul Hudā 1:144)

Shaykh Abdul Haque Muhaddith ad Dehlvi

The people of Islam have always celebrated with gatherings in the month of the Prophet's ﷺ birth. During the nights they give sadaqah, show happiness and in particular, remember the events that occurred at the time of his birth.

(Mā Thabata min asSunna p106)

Shah Walli ullah Muhaddith ad Dehlvi

I participated in a Mawlid gathering in the Honourable Makkah on the day of the Prophet's ﷺ birth. The people were sending blessings to the Prophet ﷺ, and remembering the events that occurred at the time of his birth and before his *baitha*. I then witnessed a sudden showering of *nur* upon that gathering. The *nur* was so intense that I cannot remember whether I saw it with the physical eye or the spiritual eye. Upon reflection, it became apparent to me that this nur was due to the Angels who are ordered to attend such gatherings. I also saw the mercy of Allah ﷻ descending with the *nurāni* Angels.

(Fuyooz ul Haramain 80, 81)

In another place he quotes his respected father Shah Abd ur Raheem Ad Dehlvi:

Every year I would prepare food on the occasion of the Prophet's ﷺ Mawlid. However, one year I did not have enough, so I only distributed roasted chickpeas in joy at the Prophet's ﷺ Mawlid. That night, I saw the Prophet ﷺ in a dream. He appeared very happy and before him were those chickpeas.

(Ad Dur ut Thameen 40)

Molāna Abdul Hayy Lakhnavi

Those who claim that the gathering of Mawlid is a contemptible bid'ah are acting contrary to the Shariah.

Regarding the specific date upon which the gathering is held, he writes:

There is reward for the permissible gathering of Mawlid, whenever it is held. The people of the Haramain; Basra; Syria; Yemen and other countries, after seeing the moon of Rabi ul Awwal, show happiness, organise Mawlid gatherings, do good, and read and listen to the Mawlid. Furthermore, Mawlid gatherings in these countries take place outside Rabi ul Awwal.

42

Thus one should not be of the opinion that reward for the Mawlid gathering is only in the month of Rabi ul Awwal.

(Fatāwa Abdul Hayy 2:283)

Hāji Imdād ullah Muhājir Makki[7]

All the people of the Haramain celebrate the Mawlid. That is proof enough for us. How can remembrance of the Prophet ﷺ be condemned? However, the excesses that people have devised, they should not (do so).

(Shamāim Imdādiya 87, 88)

Hāji Sahib also reveals his own practice:

The practice of (this) *faqeer* (pauper) is that he not only participates in the Mawlid gathering but sees it as a source of barakah, organises a gathering each year and finds pleasure and joy in it.

(Faisla Haft Masla p9)

Mufti Mazhar ullah Mujadidi

The reciting of the Mawlid, as long as it is based on Sahih narrations, and the procession on the blessed 12th, as long as it is free of prohibited acts, are both permissible. To call them impermissible requires proof from Shariah. What proof do the critics have against it? To simply claim that the companions of the Prophet ﷺ did not celebrate it or organise the procession in this way cannot be proof of its impermissibility. A permissible act does not become impermissible just because it was not done (before).

(Fatāwa Mazhari 435,436)

---

[7] The Shaykh and Master of Shaykh Ashraf Ali Thanvi

Allāma Muhammad Siddiq Hassan Khan Bhopālī[8]

What evil is there in someone who cannot perform the Dhikr of the Prophet ﷺ each day vowing that for one day each week or month, he will sit and perform the Dhikr and read the Sira? On top of this, he also does not leave the days of Rabi ul Awwal empty but rather reads and listens to the narrations that are proven to be sahih.

(As Shamāma tu'l Gharbiya min Khair il Mawlid alBariyya 5)

Molāna Abu Muhammad Abd al Haq Dehlvi

The Mawlid gathering, particularly in this tumultuous time, is an extremely pious act and a means of promoting Islam among the masses. As for those who undertake bid'ah in this blessed gathering, that is their fault. This accusation does not make the gathering itself bad. Building mosques and madrassas are universally good acts, but if someone undertakes bid'ahs in them, would anyone call the good acts (of building the mosques) bad? Of course not. For me, the group that have taken 'evil bid'ah' to mean the act that came into being after the third generation has committed a grave mistake.

(Taqreez bar Anwār ul Sāti'a)

Mufti Ināyat Ahmad Kākorwi

It is the practice of the Haramain and most Islamic cities to hold Mawlid gatherings in the month of Rabi ul Awwal. They gather people and narrate the events of the Prophet's ﷺ birth, recite plenty of durood, and distribute food and sweets. This act brings great barakah and is the means to increase love for the Prophet ﷺ. On the twelfth night in Madīnah, this gathering is held in the Prophet's ﷺ mosque, whilst in Makkah [it is held] in the birthplace of the Prophet ﷺ.

(Tawāreekh Habib e ilāhi)

---

[8] Widely acknowledged as the founder of the Wahhābi inspired Ahl e Hadith sect in the Indian Sub-continent

Mawlid celebrations in the blessed Haram

It is sometimes said that the Mawlid gatherings and processions are only celebrated in the Indian Sub-continent, in particular, not in the Haramain[9].

I would plead that this celebration in fact began in the Haramain; just because it is not celebrated there openly today does not mean it was never celebrated there. We will now present brief accounts of Mawlid celebrations in the Haramain.

By studying the history of the Haramain, and in particular, the books on the history of Makkah, we discover the practices of the people of the Haramain.

Visitation (Ziyāra) of the Prophet's ﷺ birthplace

It was the practice of the people of Makkah to visit the Prophet's ﷺ birthplace in the Bani Hāshim district on the night of the Mawlid. Imām Abu'l Husayn Muhammad bin Ahmad, known as Bābin Jabeer Andalusi (d614h), describes the blessed birthplace in his historic travelogue:

> Amongst the spectacles of Makkah is the Mawlid (birthplace) of the Prophet ﷺ. The dust of that place has the honour of being the first part of this world to have touched the blessed body of the Prophet ﷺ and to have the mercy for all the Ummah born upon it. On the 12th day of the month of Rabi ul Awwal, the house is opened for people to visit, which they do in great numbers and attain barakah from it.
>
> *(Rihla Ibn Jabeer 90)*

---

[9] The two sacred cities: Makkah and Madinah

He then reveals his own experience:

We entered the birthplace of the Prophet ﷺ and placed our faces on its blessed dust for that was the blessed place where this world's most blessed and pure child was born. Through this visit, we attained great barakah.

(Rihla Ibn Jabeer 126)

Imām Jamāl ud dīn Muhammad bin Jārillah writes:

On the night of the 12th of Rabi ul Awwal, after the Maghrib prayer, it has always been the practice of the people of Makkah, led by the Qādi of Makkah (who was a Shāfi'ee), to visit the birthplace [of the Prophet ﷺ] in large groups.

(Al Jāme ul Lateef 201)

Shaykh Muhammad bin Alawi Al Hassani writes:

It has always been the practice of the people of Makkah, for the Mashāikh, the grand Ulema and dignitaries, to visit the Prophet's ﷺ birthplace carrying lanterns and candles in their hands.

(Fi Rihāb Bait il Harām 262)

On seeing the (recent) destruction of the blessed birthplace of the Prophet ﷺ, Muhammad Husayn Haykal Misri decried:

Today it appears as just an empty space; sometimes it is even used as a resting place for camels. It used to be the most inhabited of all places. Those who witnessed that spectacle would be shedding tears of blood at the defilement of the Wahābies.

(Fi Manzil il Wahi 219)

46

A gathering of Dhikr would take place at the birthplace every Monday

Imām Qutbuddin Hanafi (d.988), a teacher of religious studies in Makkah, describes the practices of the people of Makkah and mentions the holding of a Dhikr gathering at the blessed birthplace every Monday:

> The blessed birthplace is very well known. It is still a place that people visit. Duas are accepted there. The people of Makkah hold a Dhikr gathering there every Monday and visit it every year on the 12th night of Rabi ul Awwal.
>
> *(Al I'lām Bi I'lām Baitillah il Harām 355)*

Mawlid Gathering at the blessed birthplace

As well as such visits (*ziyārah*), a Mawlid gathering is also held at the blessed birthplace in which the events of and signs that appeared at the time of the Prophet's ﷺ birth are remembered in great detail. Imām Qutbuddin writes:

> The people leave Masjid ul Harām in great numbers and go towards Sooq ul Lail, they congregate at the birthplace and hold a gathering there in which someone speaks.
>
> *(Al I'lām Bi I'lām Baitillah il Harām 56)*

Imām Ibn Zaheera details this gathering and describes the speech:

> A khutbah (sermon) is given in relation to that place. The people then return to Masjid ul Harām for Isha.
>
> *(Al Jāme ul Luteef 201)*

The birthplace is a place where Duas are accepted

One must always keep in mind that all of our Aslāf identified the blessed birthplace as a place whose barakah leads to the acceptance of *duas* (supplications). The Mufti of Makkah Shaykh Abdul Kareem AlQutbi (d.1014) writes:

47

Duas are accepted at the Prophet's ﷺ birthplace; it is a well-known place, located in the Bani Hāshim district.

(Al I'lām ul Ulama 154)

Distributing Food in joy of the Mawlid

It was also the practice of the people of Makkah to distribute food in celebration of the Mawlid. They would invite friends and relatives and also serve the poor and destitute, particularly the *khuddām* (servants/administrators) of the Haram. Rather than describe the practice of ordinary folk, we will focus on the practice of the Qādhi of Makkah, Imām Muhammad bin Muhiyy ud dīn At Tibri.

The famous traveller Ibn Batoota (d.728) writes in his travelogue under the heading 'The Qādi of Makkah and his Khateebs':

> The Qādi of Makkah, the Ālim, the Sālih, the Ābid, Najm udDīn Muhammad bin Imām ul Ālim Muhiyy ud dīn At Tibri distributes great sadaqah and performs a great number of tawāf around the Kabah. During the Hajj months, he distributes a great amount of food. At the time of the Prophet's ﷺ birth, in particular, he distributes food to Makkah's honourable, respected, poor, and the servants of the Haram.

> *(Rihla Ibn Batoota 1:92)*

The processions of the Makkans in joy of the Mawlid

Along with the various gatherings, the people of Makkah would also celebrate the Mawlid with illuminations and processions that were not only attended by the Ulema, Mashāikh and dignitaries but in which the ruler of the time would also participate. People would come from far away villages, even as far away as Jeddah, to participate in the gathering alongside the people of Makkah. Some would carry lanterns whilst others would be holding flags.

The procession would start at Masjid ul Harām and, after proceeding through the streets and pathways, would reach the blessed birthplace in the Bani Hāshim district, where a public gathering would be held. After that, the procession would return to Masjid ul Harām where the ruler would honour the Ulama and Mashāikh. At the end, there would be a dua and the people would return to their homes. Shaykh Qutbuddīn describes this practice:

Each year, a gathering would be announced in Masjid ul Harām for the night of the 12th of Rabi ul Awwal. The ulema, fuqahā, governors and Qādis of all the four madhabs from all areas would gather after the Maghrib prayer in Masjid ul Harām. After the prayer, they would travel through Sooq ul Lail to visit the birthplace of the Prophet ﷺ. In their hands would be a great number of lanterns, lamps and candles. There would be so many people that one could not find a place to stand. One of the scholars would speak and perform dua for all Muslims and the people would then return to Masjid ul Harām. Back at the Haram, the ruler would honour all those involved in organising the gathering. Then the Adhān and Jamāh of Isha would take place. After that, the people would return to their homes. This would be such a large gathering that people from faraway villages and towns, even as far as Jeddah, would come to participate and show their happiness.

(Al I'lām Bi I'lām Baitillah il Harām 196)

Imām Jamāludīn Muhammad bin Jārillāh writes:

It was the practice of the people of Makkah, on the 12th of Rabi ul Awwal each year, for the Qādi of Makkah – who was a Shāfi'ee – to lead a grand procession of people after the Maghrib prayer to visit the birthplace of the Prophet ﷺ. With him would be Imāms of the three (other) fiqh Madhabs, Fuqahā, Fudalā and other esteemed citizens of Makkah. In their hands they would carry lanterns and large lamps. After reaching the birthplace, there would be a sermon about the birthplace and duas for the Sultan, the Ameer of Makkah, and the Shāfi'ee Qādi. The gathering would last until just before Isha, when the people would return to Masjid ul Harām, then they would all gather at Maqām ul Ibraheem and make Dua. The Qādis and fuqaha would also participate in this. The Isha prayer would then take place and the people would depart. I do not know who

49

started this practice and even after asking contemporary historians, I still do not know.

(Al Jāme ul Lateef Fi Fadhl Makkah wa Ahliha 145/6)

21 Canon Salām

The celebrations, gatherings and processions undertaken by the people of Makkah on the day of the Mawlid in 1917 are described in the Makkan newspaper 'Al Qiblah' in the following words:

Precisely when the Muezzin called the Asr Adhān on the 11th of Rabi ul Awwal with the words 'Allah u Akbar Allah u Akbar', the walls of Makkah shook to the sound of Canon and all the people began congratulating each other on the occasion of Mawlid an Nabi. Sharif Husayn led a huge crowd in Maghrib prayer on the Hanafi Musalla in the Haram. After the prayer, the Qādi ul Qudā, as is customary, congratulated the Sharif on the occasion of Mawlid un Nabi. Then all the ministers and officers of the Sultanate and city dignitaries, along with the ordinary folk, left in a large crowd for the birthplace of the Prophet ﷺ. This splendid procession headed towards the birthplace with great pomp and ceremony. The path from the Sultan's palace to the birthplace was lit up with lights of the highest order. In particular, the birthplace was so well-lit that it would have been the envy of Jannah! After reaching it, the crowd stood with great humility. One man presented the Prophet's ﷺ Sira with great effect. After that, Shaykh Fawād, deputy foreign minister, delivered a befitting speech. At the end a Nasheed was recited that deeply moved the listeners. In the joy of Mawlid, all offices, courts and schools were closed for the day of the 12th. In this way, this day of happiness and joy came to an end. We make dua to Allah ﷻ that He shows us this day again with the same joy and happiness. Āmeen.

Nasheeds until 2 a.m!

These events were also described in the Monthly 'Tareeqat' Lahore January 1917 in the following way:

There is great happiness celebrated in Makkah on the day of the Prophet's ﷺ birth. It is known as the Day of the Prophet's ﷺ Birth. On this day, sweets are sold in great quantity. In the Haram, an elegant carpet is laid behind the Hanafi Musalla. The Shareef of Makkah and the commander of Hijāz, with their staff in splendid uniforms, come to participate. They go to the birthplace of the Prophet ﷺ and return after a short montage of nasheeds. The path between the Haram and the birthplace is lit up by a row of lanterns. The birthplace on that day resembles a dazzling light. On the way, they are led by nasheed readers who recite *na't* in sweet voices.

After the Isha prayer on the 11th of Rabi ul Awwal, a Mawlid gathering is held in the Haram. They recite Nasheed, Mowlud and Khatam until 2.a.m. During that night, many different processions go to the birthplace and recite Nasheeds. From the Maghrib prayer on the 11th to the Asr prayer on the 12th, a 21 Canon salute is given at each prayer. During these days, the Makkans rejoice greatly, recite Nasheed and hold many Mawlid gatherings.

Greater fervour than Eid

Imām Sakhāwi writes that the people of Makkah show greater endeavour for the Mawlid than they do for Eid, and all of them visit the birthplace:

> The people of Makkah visit the birthplace – which is authenticated and is in Sooq ul Lail – in the hope that their needs will be fulfilled. And they celebrate it more so than Eid. On this day, everyone visits the birthplace, whether he be pious or not, fortunate or unfortunate.
>
> *(Al Mawrid arRawā 28)*

The Practices of the People of Madīnah

Having considered the people of Makkah, let us now look at the practices of the people of Madīnah:

Shaykh ul Muhadditheen Mulla Ali Qāri (d.1014), after mentioning the practices of the rest of the world's Muslims on the day of the Mawlid, writes:

> The people of Madīnah – may Allah ﷻ give them greater success – hold many gatherings and participate in them in great numbers.
>
> *(Al Mawrid arRawā 29)*

If only I could hold a gathering on each day of Rabi ul Awwal!

After describing the practices of the Aslāf, he writes about the Imām of the time, Shaykh Abu Isāq bin Abd ur Rehman:

> When he was in Madīnah – may there be great blessings and perfect praise upon its resident – he would celebrate the Mawlid, distribute food to the people and say 'If I were able I would do the same on each day of Rabi ul Awwal'.

The practice of Mulla Ali Qāri

Mulla Ali Qāri then explains that his financial position does not allow him to feed others, so instead he is writing a book which will benefit people until the end of time:

> I plead that this pauper is too weak to serve the people in the material sense, but in order to serve them in a symbolic and *nurāni* sense, I have written this book to quench people's thirst on this Earth until the end of time and have named it *al mawrid ar rawā fi'l mawlid an nabawi* (The means to quench the thirsty in Mawlid un Nabawi).
>
> *(Al Mawrid arRawā 32)*

The Mawlid gathering would be held in Masjid un Nabawi

In describing the practices of the people of the Haramain, Mufti Inayat Ahmad Kākorwi writes:

52

On the 12th of Rabi ul Awwal, this blessed gathering of the Prophet ﷺ would take place in Masjid un Nabawi in Madīnah and at the birthplace in Makkah.

(Tawāreekh Habeeb e Ilāhi 15)

Description of a Mawlid gathering in Masjid un Nabawi in 1287

Molāna Abd ul Haq Ala Abādi writes that he saw his Shaykh and Murshid, Umda tu'l Mufassireen and Zubda tul Muhadditheen, Shah Abdul A'la Naqshbandi Mujadidi:

> participating in the Mawlid gathering held in the Prophet's ﷺ Mosque on the 12th of Rabi ul Awwal 1287 hijri. The gathering was in the courtyard of the Mosque and the Ulema sat at the pulpit facing the blessed tomb and spoke on the Mawlid of the Prophet ﷺ. During the remembrance, the time to rise came. The atmosphere, events and barakah that appeared at that gathering cannot be expressed in speech or writing.

(Ad Durr ul Munazzam 113)

Is the Mawlid gathering a Bid'ah?

Some people, sometimes rather vocally, object to the organisation and celebration of the Mawlid and its gathering.

As mentioned before, the Mawlid gathering is the name given to the gathering in remembrance of Allah ﷻ and of the Prophet ﷺ, both of which are the foundations, essence and fruits of Islamic teachings. Each element of this gathering is mentioned in the texts of the Quran and Sunnah. Consequently, to slander it as Bid'ah and contrary to the teachings of Islam is excessive, and indeed an affront to Islam. Unfortunately, despite this, a small minority still insists on criticising this blessed gathering. Thus it is necessary to discuss this issue.

First of all it is important to understand the definition of bid'ah, so that we can appraise whether the Mawlid gathering is bid'ah or not.

Bid'ah literally means a new affair; a new mode; a new tradition or ritual. Imām Nawawi defines it as:

A thing that has no previous example.

(Shara Sahih Muslim Nawawi 1.285)

Hāfiz Ibn Hajar states:

Literally Bid'ah is that which is invented without a previous example.

(Fath ul Bāri 4:219)

An attribute of Allah ﷻ is mentioned in the Quran as:

He initiated the skies and the lands without a model and when he decides on a task, He says *Kun*, and it becomes (6:73)

Here the word Bid'ah is in its literal sense; Allah ﷻ created the skies and the land without an earlier example or model. In another place, our Prophet ﷺ is told:

Say: 'I am not an innovation among the Messengers' (46:9)

The Prophet ﷺ is told to explain that he is a messenger like the other messengers; his teachings are the same as those of previous messengers.

However, the people of knowledge concur that the bid'ah that is vilified and condemned in the Quran and Hadith is not the literal bid'ah but the bid'ah as defined specifically by Shariah (Shar'ī Bid'ah). Remember that whenever the Quran and Sunnah use a word, they do not use its literal meaning but restrict it to its Shar'ī meaning. For example, Salah has many literal meanings, such as supplication and the burning of fire, but its Shar'ī meaning is Prayer and the performance of certain predetermined tasks (Ruku, Sajdah etc). Similarly, Hajj has many literal meanings; intention, motive etc., but its Shar'ī meaning is the performance of certain rituals in a specified place at a specified time. The term bid'ah is used in the same way. Therefore, it is necessary to define and understand the Shar'ī meaning of bid'ah.

Shar'ī Meaning of Bid'ah

Every addition or reduction in religion for which there is no proof in Shariah. If a belief or new action has a Shar'ī basis, it is most definitely not a (Shar'ī) bid'ah.

This definition was established by our beloved Prophet ﷺ. Syeduna Jareer bin Abdullah narrates the following saying of the Prophet ﷺ:

Whoever begins a good thing in Islam will receive the reward of all those who imitate (copy) it, without there being a reduction in the reward of the imitators. And whoever initiates a bad thing in Islam will receive the sin of all the imitators without a reduction in their sin.

(Sahih Muslim)

55

In another hadith narrated by Syeduna Abu Hurayra, the Prophet ﷺ said:

Whoever calls [others] to (the path of) guidance and good will receive the reward of those who follow it with no reduction in their (the followers) reward, and whoever calls to deviation (and wrong) will have the sin of those following it without any reduction in their sin.

(Sahih Muslim)

These narrations provide us with the principle that any act that does not defy the spirit and thought of Shariah is good, and so initiating and imitating such acts is also good. Conversely, initiating and imitating acts that are contrary to the spirit of Shariah is catastrophic. In reference to these ahadith, Imām Shāmi writes:

The people of knowledge state that a basic ruling of Islam is established from these ahadith, that each person who invents a bad [action] receives the sin of all those re-enacting that bad [action], whilst the one who initiates a good [action] receives the reward of all those imitating it, until the day of Qiyāmah.

(Muqaddima Fatāwa Shāmi)

In summary, acts that are within the rules and principles of Shariah are permissible whilst those that counter the rules and regulations of Shariah are impermissible. This is the Shar'ī meaning of bid'ah that our aslāf have been espousing to this day.

Our Aslāf and the meaning of Bid'ah

Shaykh Ibn Rajab Hanbali states:

The meaning of bid'ah is a new act that is without Shar'ī proof. New acts for which there is Shar'ī proof are not Shar'ī bid'ah, even if they are literal bid'ah.

(Jāme Ul Uloom Wal Hikam)

In explaining the Prophet's ﷺ proclamation, 'The worst actions are those that are invented', Imām Badr ud dīn Aini states:

Each new work which has no Shar'ī basis is an invention and is known in Shari'ah as Bid'ah, and any act that does have a Shar'ī basis is not a Bid'ah.

(Umda tul Qāri)

Hāfīz Ibn Hajar's concluding remarks are:

The truth is this that if the new act comes within a Shar'ī good action then it is good and if it comes under a Shar'ī bad action, then it is disliked. .

(Fath ul Bāri 4:219)

Allāma Sād ud dīn Taftazāni (d.792h) defines a contemptible Bid'ah as:

Each new invention is a bid'ah if it was not found in the time of the Sahāba and Tābi'een and for which there is no Shar'ee proof.

(Iqāma tul Hujja from Shara Maqāsid fi ilm-il-kalām 2.271)

Molāna Abdul Hayy Lakhnavi writes:

Every new action invented after the (first) three generations will be assessed against the evidence of Shariah - if there exists an example of it in the first three periods or if it comes under Sharī rulings then it is not bid'ah - because bid'ah refers to inventions that are neither found in the first three generations nor come under Shar'ee reasoning.

(Iqāma t'ul Hujja)

While discussing bid'ah *hasana* (good) and bid'ah *sa'īyya* (evil), Molāna Muhammad Sarfarāz Khān Deobandi states:

There are two types of bid'ah - literal and shar'ī. Literal bid'ah is that which was invented after the passing away of the Prophet ﷺ, whether it is in worship or ritual, and there are 5 types (of them): Wājib, Mandoob, Harām, Makruh and Mubah. Shar'ī bid'ah is that which is not found in the first three generations and for which the legislator's permission cannot be found in either his statements or actions, either explicitly or implicitly. This is the bid'ah that is known as Dalāla, Qabeeha and Sa'īyya.

(Rāh e Sunnah 99)

Thus far, it is clear that any new matter that comes under Shar'ī principles is permissible and any that do not have such a basis, either in words or actions, explicitly or implicitly, are wrong and impermissible.

The mistaken definition of Bid'ah

Some people define bid'ah simply as a new action that the companions did not undertake. They do not check if it falls under Shar'ī rulings or not. It should be clear by now from the above discussion that such a simplistic definition is both inadequate and wrong. However, it is important to mention the clarifications of our Aslāf who deemed such a definition as ignorant. While discussing bid'ah, Allāma Taftazāni writes:

> Those people who call each new action not found in the time of the Sahāba a contemptible bid'ah, even though there is no condemnation of it in Shari'ah, are ignorant. Their reasoning is based on the Prophet's ﷺ call to refrain from inventions but they do not know that this statement only refers to those inventions that have no place in the religion.
>
> *(Shara ul Maqāsid 2.271)*

Molāna Abdul Hayy Lakhnavi states:

> A section of the Ulama of our time are wrong, and belong to two groups; one restricts the Sunnah to only those actions that occurred in the [first] three generations and label all actions after that (time) bid'ah and deviant, without bothering to inspect whether or not such actions come under any principle of Shari'ah. Some in this group even restrict the Sunnah to just the

lifetime of the Prophet ﷺ and view the new practices of the Sahāba as bid'ah! Whereas the other group are those who adopt every action of their forefathers and in this way denote many bid'ah sa'īyya acts as bid'ah hasana, without there being any shar'ī proof for those actions.

(Iqāma tul Hujja 7)

Is the Mawlid Gathering Bid'ah?

The principal component of the Mawlid gathering is the remembrance *(dhikr)* of the Prophet ﷺ. Consequently, objections to this gathering seem very strange especially when *Dhikr-ul-Rasool* is not contrary to the teachings of Islam but is one of the foundations of Islam. There are rulings for it in the Shari'ah, in statements and actions, explicitly and implicitly. It is the same dhikr that occurs in the heavens and that same dhikr which Allah, the all Powerful, elevated. It is incomprehensible that one cannot find a Shar'ī proof for it! Is there no example of it in the times of the Sahāba and Tābi'een? Is the command to rejoice when we receive Allah's ﷻ *fadhl* and *rahmah* not from the scriptures? Has the Ummah not been given the command {and mention the blessings of your Lord}? What was the purpose of announcing {Verily Allah favoured the believers when he sent a messenger to them}? Did the Prophet ﷺ teach us nothing by fasting on a Monday?!

It is necessary for every Muslim to reflect if, in his obstinacy, he is acting against the Quran and Sunnah.

Views regarding the Mawlid gathering

Let us inspect the statements of the scholars who determined the Shar'ī meaning of bid'ah on the Mawlid gathering (in the following accounts, Mawlid gathering refers to organising gatherings, preparing food etc., because it is widely assumed that *Dhikr-ul-Rasool* is the basis of Islam).

Imām Hāfiz Abu Muhammad Abd ur Rehmān Shahāb ud dīn Abu Shāma Muqaddasi Shafi'ī (d.665), who reached the rank of ijtihad, wrote a whole book on bid'ah entitled *'Al Bā'ith Ala Inkār ul*

59

bid'ah wal havādis' in which he clarified that the Mawlid gathering is not bid'ah, and if one must call it bid'ah, it should be called bid'ah hasana:

> In our time in the city of Irbil, the sadaqah, show of splendour and happiness displayed on the day of the Prophet's ﷺ birth, comes under the category of bid'ah hasana. (This is) because through it, not only are the poor fed, but love and respect for the Prophet ﷺ is expressed and thanks is given to Allah ﷻ for granting us His Prophet, the mercy for all the worlds.
>
> *(Al Bā'ith Ala Inkārul bid'ah wal havādis)*

Imām Jalāludīn Suyooti in the commentary of Sunan Ibn Majah states:

> The correct view is that the Mawlid gathering is bid'ah *hasana mandooba* (a good, permissible act) as long as it is free from prohibited acts.
>
> *(Subl ul Hudā)*

Imām Zaheer ud dīn Ja'far Misri writes:

> The Mawlid gathering is bid'ah hasana when our purpose is to gather the Sāliheen, send Salawāt and Durood upon the Prophet ﷺ and feed the poor and destitute.
>
> *(Subl ul Hudā)*

As has been illustrated in previous chapters, for over a thousand years, leading scholars have demonstrated, with evidence, that the Mawlid gathering is a good act. To call it deviant, therefore, is clearly excessive, for there is no scope to object to it after reading these statements.

Scholars who have objected to the Mawlid gathering have not objected to the gathering itself but rather to the illegal acts that a minority of ignorant people include in it. A close study of their texts will reveal this. Although one must recognise and condemn such illicit acts as bad, it is regrettable that some declare the entire remembrance of the Prophet ﷺ to be bid'ah.

Critics should read the work of Imām Ibn ul Hāj, who condemns these illicit acts but also encourages the honouring of day of the birth and the month of Rabi ul Awwal:

> The Prophet ﷺ was asked about the Fast on a Monday to which he replied, 'On this day I was born'. Through this statement, the Prophet ﷺ established the high status of the month in which the day of his birth occurred. Thus, we should treat this month with great respect. This also reveals that a time and place do not have innate or intrinsic virtues[10] but rather they owe their status to the events (that occurred in that place or time). May Allah ﷻ have mercy on all of us. O reader! Look at the status of this month and the day Monday – both of whom Allah ﷻ selected for the arrival of the Prophet ﷺ!
>
> *(Al Mudkhal)*

---

[10] Are not virtuous for their own sakc or their personal qualities.

Is the Day of Mawlid an Eid?

A small minority object to using the word Eid in conjunction with the Mawlid of the Prophet ﷺ. They argue it is inappropriate because there are only two Eids in Islam, Adha and Fitr, and both contain a special prayer.

It will become clear that in the light of the Quran and Sunnah, the above criticism is invalid. The Quran itself has denoted days other than Fitr and Adha as Eid.

Eid refers to a day of happiness and what could be more joyful for Muslims than the day on which the mercy for all creation came into this world! To understand what Eid is, inspect the following supplication made by Syeduna Isa عليه السلام:

> O our Lord, send us from heaven a table set, that there may be for us – the first and the last of us – an Eid (a solemn festival)
>
> *(Quran 5:114)*

Imām Fakhr ud dīn Rāzi writes in the tafsīr of this verse:

> (It means) O Allah, we will deem that day Eid on which you will send down a tablespread. We will honour that day and so will those who follow us. That tablespread was sent down on a Sunday, and so the Christians made that day their Eid.

For his whole ummah, Syeduna Isa عليه السلام is labelling as an Eid the day on which Allah ﷻ will shower them with His blessings. But for us Muslims, what can be a greater blessing than the arrival of the Prophet ﷺ, who brought humanity out of ignorance? If that day is not an Eid, then what day is? All other Eids were only received as a result of this day!

Some may argue that labelling such days as Eid is a practice of earlier nations and should not be taken as a precedent for Muslims. Such a criticism simply braves the ignorance of the antagonists because the events of earlier nations narrated to us are, unless Islam declares them to be wrong, a source of guidance. However, we shall endeavour to prove that one can also refer to days other than Adha and Fitr as Eid. Syeduna Abu Hurayra narrates that he heard the Prophet ﷺ say:

> The day of Friday is an Eid. Thus you should not fast on this day of Eid unless you are fasting before or after it.
>
> *(Al Mustadrak 1:603)*

Syeduna Abu Hurayra also narrates that in one year, Eid occurred on a Friday and the Prophet ﷺ said to the companions:

> Today you have two Eids combined.
>
> *(Al Mustadrak, Book of Jumuah)*

About this hadith, Shaikh Abdul Qādir Atta refers to Imām Dhahabi's statement 'they are Sahih and Gareeb'.

Syeduna Ayās bin Abi Ramla Shāmi narrates that one day, he went to Syeduna Mu'awiyya, who asked Syeduna Zaid who was seated with him:

> 'Were you ever with the Prophet ﷺ when two Eids occurred on the same day?'
> He replied, 'Yes'.
> The hadith goes on to explain that it was both an Eid and a Friday.
>
> *(Al Mustadrak, Book of Jumuah)*

Friday is better than the two Eids of Adha & Fitr

The Prophet ﷺ did not just denote Friday as an Eid but taught that it was better than Eid ul Fitr and Adha! Syeduna Abu Lubāba bin Abd ul Manzar narrates that the Prophet ﷺ said:

> Friday is the Chief (sayyid) of all days and to Allah is the most revered and better than both the day of Adha and the day of Fitr.
>
> *(Mishkāt ul Masābih, Bāb ul Jumuah)*

The ahadith also reveal why Friday is so honoured. On Friday, Allah ﷻ created Syeduna Adam ﷺ for His worship and on the other days, He created the things humans use. As it is so necessary to thank Allah ﷻ for the blessing of existence (for it is the source of all other blessings), the ibādah of that day is better than the ibādah of other days. Syeduna Oas bin Oas narrates that the Prophet ﷺ said about Friday:

> From your days, Friday is the best; on it Syeduna Adam was born and on it he passed away.
>
> *(Abu Dawud, Nisai, Ibn Majah, Dārmi)*

Syeduna Abu Hurayra narrates that the Prophet ﷺ was asked why Friday is called Jumuah, and he replied:

> On it your father Adam's mould was made, on it Qiyāmah will be instituted, on it you will be raised again and in it there is a time when Allah ﷻ accepts all supplications.
>
> *(Mishkāt ul Masābih from Musnad Ahmad)*

Reflect carefully; the day on which Syeduna Adam ﷺ was created is greater than not only the other days of the week but also the two Eids! It includes a time when Allah ﷻ accepts all supplications, so it is obvious that this special time must be when Syeduna Adam ﷺ was created. Thus, one can only wonder at the status of the day and time at which the Prophet of all the prophets and the reason for all of creation was born!

64

The dua at the time of the Prophet's ﷺ birth

Imām Ibn ul Hāj, after mentioning that the dua of Muslims is accepted at the time of Syeduna Adam's ﷺ creation each Friday, ponders the scope of Allah's ﷻ acceptance at the time corresponding to the birth of His ﷻ beloved:

> There is no doubt that the one who finds the time of the Prophet's ﷺ birth and supplicates [to Allah ﷻ] will definitely be successful in his wish. This is because, if the time in Jumuah when Syeduna Adam ﷺ was created is a time of acceptance, what is the state of the hour in which *the chief of the first and last* was born?

He then mentions another prominent difference between the day of Jumuah and the day of Mawlid:

> Syeduna Adam ﷺ was also born on it (Friday), he was sent to the Earth that day, and Qiyāmah will take place on it, however the day of Monday[11] is purely peaceful and good.

(Al Mudhkal)

The day of Arafah is Eid

The labelling of Eid is not just restricted to Friday. Islam declared *Yowm al Arafah* (9th day of Dhul Hajj) as an Eid. In Tirmidhi, Syeduna Abdullah Ibn Abāss narrates that when the Prophet ﷺ recited the verse {Today I have completed for you your religion}, some Jewish men were sitting nearby and commented:

> Had this verse been revealed to us we would have declared that day an Eid. On hearing this, the Prophet ﷺ replied, 'You would only have celebrated one Eid; we had two Eids when this was revealed! One being Friday and the other being the day of Arafah.'

(Tirmidhi, Tafsir Sura Al Māida)

---

[11] The day of the Prophet's ﷺ birth.

Imām Khāzin narrates from Ibn Abbās that on that day, there
were 5 Eids!   *(Lubāb uTtāweel)*

Sahih Bukhāri contains a similar account; a Jewish man said to
Syeduna Umar that the latter's holy book had a verse which, if it had
been revealed to them (the Jews), they would have celebrated that day
as an Eid.

Syeduna Umar asked which verse and was told, {Today I have
completed for you your religion}, to which he replied:

> We know the time and place of its revelation to our Prophet ﷺ.
> He was standing at Arafah and it was a Friday.
>
> *(Bukhāri)*

Imām Aini and Imām Nawawi explain this reply:

> It means we also respect that time and that place, as the place
> was Arafah, where the biggest ritual of Hajj takes place, and the
> time was both Friday and the day of Arafah, thus two greatness'
> are combined in that time, and as respecting each one is
> compulsory for all Muslims, when two come together, the
> respect increases further. Thus we have made that day an Eid.
>
> *(Umda tul Qāri 1:264)*

If Friday is an Eid then Muslims have at least four Eids each month in
which they can express their happiness. Yet some still insist on
rejecting the notion of a third Eid! One will have noticed from the
above discussion that the day on which a verse is revealed can become
as many as 5 Eids, so why should the day on which the being that is
the personification of the Quran was sent to this world not also be an
Eid? One fails to understand why objections are raised to calling such
a day an Eid!

Days of Tashreeq are Eid

One should also be aware that the days of Tashreeq are Eid for
Muslims. Syeduna Uqba bin Āmir narrates that the Prophet ﷺ said:

The days of Arafah, Sacrifice and Tashreeq are Eids for us and are days of eating and drinking.

(Al Mustadrak 1:600)

Friday night is better than Lail a'tul Qadr

Leading Imāms and Scholars, in particular Imam Ahmad bin Hanbal, have taught that not only is Friday an Eid but its night is also better than *Lail a tul Qadr* as it was during a Friday night that the celebrated nur of the Prophet ﷺ appeared in the blessed and pure womb of Syeda Āminah. Shaykh Fath ullah Banāni narrates Imām Ahmad ibn Hanbal's statement:

Friday night is better than *Lail a tul Qadr* because on this night the pure and blessed nur appeared in the blessed womb of Syeda Āminah.

(Mawlid Khair Khalqillah 158)

Shaykh Abd al Haque Muhaddith ad Dehlvi writes:

It was narrated by Imām Ibn Hanbal that Friday night is better than the night of Qadr because on this night the blessed nur of the Prophet ﷺ - which is the cause of innumerable blessings and virtues - appeared in the pure womb of Syeda Āminah.

(Isha t'ul Lumāt 1:577)

Shaykh Ashraf Ali Thānwi also writes:

It was narrated by Imām Ahmad that Friday night has a greater status than the night of Qadr because on this night the Prophet ﷺ appeared in the pure womb of his mother Syeda Āminah. And the Prophet's ﷺ arrival was the cause of so much goodness and blessing for both this and the next world that it is impossible to measure.

(Juma ke fazāil wa ahkām)

If the night in which the Prophet's ﷺ nur appeared in Syeda Āminah's womb is better than the night of Qadr, then imagine the status of the

67

day on which the Prophet ﷺ appeared to the whole world! Would that day not be greater than Eid?

The Aslāf and the use of the word Eid

Evidence that the Aslāf termed the day of Mawlid as a day of happiness (i.e. Eid, as Eid means a day of happiness) exists and some of it is presented below.

Imām Jalāludīn Suyooti narrates an event about a Māliki scholar called Abul Tayyib Muhammad bin Ibrahim Al-Busti (d.395) who passed by a madrassa on the 12th of Rabi ul Awwal and went up to the teacher and said:

> O *faqih*, today is a day of happiness so give the children a holiday.
>
> *(Al hāwi lil fatāwa 1:197)*

Imām Qustalāni (d.911), who wrote a commentary on Sahih Bukhāri, details the activities of Rabi-ul-Awwal - the organisation of the gathering of Mawlid, the giving of Sadaqah, the relaying of the life of the Prophet ﷺ - and then supplicates:

> May Allah ﷻ bless each and every one who celebrates the nights of the month of Mawlid as Eid and thereby casts affliction upon the one with sickness (of opposition to Mawlid) in his heart.
>
> *(Al Muwāhib Ludduniya 1:148)*

Shaikh Fath ullah Banāni Misri narrates the following saying of the Aslāf about the Mawlid:

> Because of this day, Allah ﷻ gave this Ummah greater status over the other Ummahs. Thus it is necessary for this Ummah to celebrate this night as the greatest Eid.
>
> *(Mawlid Khair Khalq illah)*

Some critics argue that if Mawlid is an Eid, why is there no special prayer for it, as there is with the other Eids. To understand the reason, one needs to delve into the realms of honour and love. Muhadditheen and Mufassireen, through their knowledge of the Quran and Sunnah, provided the reason some 700 years ago. Here, just two universally-accepted scholars will be cited.

Imām Ibn ul Hāj (d.737) states that the great blessing in the form of the Prophet ﷺ should make it compulsory for us to offer extra worship by way of gratitude, however it is due to Allah's ﷻ mercy – embedded in the Prophet ﷺ – that additional worship has not been demanded.

> The reason for this is the Prophet's ﷺ mercy and kindness towards his ummah. It is for this same reason that the Prophet ﷺ would refrain from or cease many acts in fear that they may become compulsory for the Ummah. Allah ﷻ mentions the Prophet's ﷺ kindness in the Quran; that he is very merciful and kind to the believers.[12]
>
> *(Al Mudhkal 2:2)*

He then asks the above question rhetorically, before answering it:

> If one was to ask that Fridays have an extra prayer and sermon, and if (the Mawlid) is better, why does it not have an extra worship, the answer is as mentioned before; whilst seeking to lighten (the burden on) his Ummah, he did not introduce an additional ibādah nor demand one from his ummah. Thus when Allah ﷻ gave the Prophet ﷺ his physical body on this day, it was in honour of the Prophet ﷺ that He did not make any extra (ibādah) compulsory. Allah ﷻ termed the Prophet ﷺ a mercy for all worlds. This mercy is generally for all of creation but is most specifically for his Ummah. Amongst his kindness and mercy is the fact that Allah ﷻ did not order extra worship on the day of his birth.
>
> *(Al Mudkhal 2:30)*

---

[12] Verse 9:128: 'Surely, a Messenger has come unto you from among yourselves; grievous to him is it that you should fall into trouble; he is ardently desirous of your welfare; and to the believers he is especially compassionate and merciful.'

Imām Ahmad Qustalāni (d.923) also answers this objection while discussing the status of the night of the Mawlid:

If Fridays, on which Syeduna Adam ﷺ was born, contain a time when a Muslim has any dua accepted, then what of that time when the chief of all prophets arrived? The reason the day of Mawlid does not have an extra prayer or khutbah, as Fridays do, is out of respect for the Prophet's ﷺ merciful status that the burden on his Ummah be lightened. Allah ﷻ says, 'We have not sent you but as a mercy for all the worlds' and one of the expressions of this mercy is that no extra worship was made compulsory.

(Al Muwāhib ul Ludduniya 1:142)

No word can describe this day

All the references presented so far have made clear that there is no day greater than the day of his ﷺ birth. No Jumuah or day of Eid can rival it. If we were to reflect upon its greatness then even the word Eid is not worthy of it. However, we have no better word than this and so we must suffice with the word Eid. How wonderfully Shaykh Muhammad Alawi Māliki stated that although the joys of Eid come and go, the happiness (Eid) that the arrival of the Prophet ﷺ brought to Allah's ﷻ creation is eternal.

We do not give the Prophet's ﷺ day the name of Eid because it is much greater than Eid! The two Eids we have in Islam - Eid ul Fitr and Eid ul Adha - come once a year but his remembrance is much more elevated than this, because it does not take place once or even twice a year, but rather it is appropriate for the Muslim to live his whole life in remembrance of him ﷺ, loving him, acting upon his sunnah and having a connection with him.

(Al Mawrid aw Rawā)

If one keeps this narrative in mind, many things will automatically be resolved. In summary, remembrance of the Prophet ﷺ is good and a source of barakah and good fortune. Whoever is apportioned any of this will feel Allah's ﷻ *fadhl* and favour upon him.

70

However, it is obligatory for the organisers of Mawlid gatherings to ensure that they are protected from illegal acts so that no one points an accusing finger at this blessed gathering because of a few bad deeds. As for its critics, they should raise their voice against evil but they should not make the very gathering the subject of their criticism, because it is purely in remembrance of the Prophet ﷺ, who is extremely beloved to Allah ﷻ Himself.

May Allah ﷻ give us all the ability to tread the path of moderation.

Four possible objections to the narration by Syeduna Abbās

When one mentions the narration by Syeduna Abbās of Abu Lahab's condition in the grave, four possible objections may be raised:

1. The narration is Mursal[13] and is thus not admissible as evidence.
2. It relates to a dream and so cannot prove anything.
3. The narration contradicts Quranic verses.
4. Thowbiya was freed by Abu Lahab after the migration and not at the time of the Prophet's ﷺ birth.

Before reviewing these objections, one should keep in mind that this narration is not the basis, or even the proof, of the Mawlid gathering, for we have already given evidence of it from the Quran and Sunnah. This narration is mentioned merely to support the scriptural evidence.

We will now discuss each of these objections in turn:

This narration is not admissible because it is Mursal

In response to this objection we will simply present the statements of the great Imāms and allow the reader to make up their own mind over the acceptability or not of a Mursal narration.

---

[13] This term relates to the hadith's chain of transmission. It is a chain that goes back to a Tābi'ee, and does not mention the name of the Prophet's ﷺ companion that the Tābi'ee heard it from. A Tābi'ee is someone who saw a companion but not the Prophet ﷺ.

One must remember that all four Imāms of Fiqh - Imām Abu Haneefa, Imām Mālik, Imām Shāfi'ee and Imām Ahmad bin Hanbal - all agree that a Mursal hadith is acceptable. Three of them accept it unconditionally, while Imām Shāfi'ee does so conditionally. The hāfiz of Hadith Jalāl ud dīn Suyooti quotes Ibn Jareer:

> The Tābi'een reached ijma (consensus) on the acceptance of the Mursal, and no rejection from any of them is narrated and nor from any of the Imāms 200 years after them.
>
> *(Tadreeb ur Rāwi)*

Imām Nawawi, the commentator of Sahih Muslim, writes about the Mursal narration:

> The *madhab* (school) of Imām Mālik, Abu Haneefa, Ahmad and most of the jurists states that it (Mursal) is acceptable as evidence, whereas the *madhab* of Imām Shāfi'ee holds that the Mursal, when confirmed by something else, is acceptable as evidence.
>
> *(Muqaddima of Imām Muslim)*

Shaykh Abdul Haque Muhaddith ad Dehlvi mentions this position of the Imāms in the following words:

> For Imām Abu Haneefa and Mālik, a Mursal is unconditionally acceptable. Their reasoning is that it is transmitted on the basis of trust and reputation, as this matter concerns *thiqa* (trustworthy) people. If the narration was not sahih according to its *thiqa* narrator, he (the narrator) would never have claimed the Prophet ﷺ had said it. For Imām Shāfi'ee, if the Mursal can be confirmed in any other way then it will be acceptable. There are two statements by Imām Ahmad; according to one it is acceptable and according to the other it is *tawaqquf*.

Shaykh Jamāl ud dīn Qāsimi mentions three statements about the Mursal, the second of which is:

It was said by Abu Haneefa and Mālik that the Mursal is unconditional evidence. According to Imām Nawawi, this is also the view of Ahmad, Ibn Qayyim and Ibn Katheer.

(Qawāid ul Tahdeeth)

Doctor Mahmud Al Tahhān, of Shariah College Islamic University Madīnah, mentions three statements, of which the second and third are:

The second statement is that a Mursal is sahih and acceptable as evidence according to the three Imāms; Abu Haneefa, Mālik and Ahmad. Imām Ahmad's famous statement is that (it is acceptable) if the narrator is *thiqa* and he narrates from a *thiqa* narrator. The rationale is: how could a thiqa Tābi'ee claim it is from the Prophet ﷺ unless he heard it from a thiqa person?!
The third statement is that it is acceptable with conditions. This is the view of Imām Shāfi'ee and some other people of knowledge.

(Taiseer Mustalih ul Hadith)

This text reveals that although there are two statements by Imām Hanbal regarding the Mursal, the most well-known is that it is acceptable. The following words of Imām Suyooti also support this:

The well-known statement of Imām Mālik, Abu Haneefa and Ahmad is that it is sahih (authentic).

(Tadreeb ur Rāwi)

As for the claim that the muhadditheen do not accept it, the simple response is to ask whether any muhaddith is greater than these four Imāms? These Imāms are not just muhaddith but are mujtahids and faqeeh, whose views are stronger and superior to the muhaddith in all cases.

Furthermore, to claim that the muhadditheen do not accept the Mursal under any circumstance is also contentious, because Imām Abu Dawud, who is a great muhaddith, writes:

74

As for the Mursal, verily most of the ulema have used it as evidence, for example Sufyān Thowri, Mālik, Owzāi'ee, until Imām Shafi'ee came and disagreed, and then Imām Ahmad and others followed him.

(Risāla Abu Dawud ila ahl i Makka)

The truth is that the viewpoint of the muhadditheen is the same as that of Imām Shāfi'ee.

The balanced view of the Mursal

We have presented all of the statements above to clarify the position of the Mursal, although our view concurs with those ulema who hold the moderate opinion; that if the transmitter is known to be narrating from someone who is known to be *thiqa*, the narration is acceptable. If it isn't, then it is not.

Comprehensive research on this topic was undertaken by Hāfiz Salāh ud dīn Abu Saeed Khalil bin Kaikaldi Alāi (d761), who writes that there are ten statements regarding the Mursal, and describes the most accepted opinion in the following words:

The seventh is that if the transmitter was known to only narrate from famously thiqa people, then it is accepted. If not, then [it is] not [accepted], and this is the *mukhtār* (preferred) opinion.

It is for this reason that Imām Shāfi'ee, who initially disagreed over the Mursal, had to concede that the Mursal narration of Saeed ibn Musayyab was acceptable to him because he only transmitted narrations from thiqa people. Shaykh Qaffāl Muroozi narrates about Imām Shāfi'ee:

The Mursal (transmission) of Ibn Musayyab is evidence for us.

(Jāme ut Tahseel fi ahkām il Marāseel)

This is only a dream

The second objection is that this narration is about a dream and a dream cannot be proof. In response, we agree that a dream of a non-

75

prophet is not legal evidence, but we do not present this narration as the *only* evidence but as support and confirmation of other evidence. Furthermore, there is no such principle that states that such narrations have no benefit at all:

Firstly, the Quran presents the dream of a non-Muslim as true and a source of some valuable insight. It is said in Sura Yusuf that two prison companions of Syeduna Yusuf had a dream, which they mentioned to him, who interpreted them and found them to be true. After hearing their dreams, Syeduna Yusuf invited them to Tawheed and Imān, revealing that both of them were in a state of unbelief at the time[14].

Secondly, there are two separate matters here; one, that Syeduna Abbās saw the dream in which Abu Lahab said that his punishment is reduced on a Monday because of the barakah of freeing Thowbiya, and two, whilst awake, Syeduna Abbās also said:

And (the reason for it is) the Prophet ﷺ was born on a Monday and Thowbiya gave Abu Lahab the good news and he freed her.

(Fath ul Bāri)

Thus, this is not just a dream but is a statement made by a companion of the Prophet ﷺ, an interpreter of the Quran which, because of it being something underived or uninferred, holds the rank of Marfooh[15].

Thirdly, if, Allah ﷻ forbidding, this was a false dream, Syeduna Abbās would never have mentioned it, and even if he had, the other companions and Tābi'een would have rejected it. However, no such suspicion of its truthfulness is found in the books of ahadith, rather, it is quoted by all and used as evidence.

One other possible objection at this juncture could be that the statement of Syeduna Abbās is unreliable for, at the time, he was not

---

[14] The Quran 12: 36-41

[15] This relates to the classification of ahadith in terms of who the text is attributed to. A Marfooh narration is that which is attributed to the Prophet ﷺ himself. A Moqoof hadith is one where the text is attributed to a companion (or in which it doesn't explicitly state that the Prophet ﷺ himself said those words).

a Muslim. Firstly, this is incorrect as he had accepted Islam by the time he had this dream, two years after Badr; Abu Lahab died one year after Badr and met Abbās in a dream one year after his death. When Syeduna Abbās came to take part in Badr, the Prophet ﷺ said to his companions:

> Whoever meets Abbās bin Abdul Muttalib should not kill him because he has been compelled to come out.
>
> *(al kāmil fi Tāreekh)*

This is also supported by the episode in which the prisoners of Badr were being freed and *fidya* was being sought. Syeduna Abbās claimed that he had nothing and the Prophet ﷺ remarked, 'O uncle, tell us of the wealth you gave Umm e Fadhl?'
Syeduna Abbās replied:

> By the one who sent you with the truth, no one except me and my wife know about this and so I know that you are the messenger of Allah.
>
> *(al kāmil fi Tāreekh)*

Secondly, even if we accept that he was in a state of kufr at that time, the narration is still acceptable because what matters is that he was a Muslim at the time of the narration, rather than at the time of the event. It is beyond doubt that when the Tābi'een heard this narration from him, he was a Muslim. The muhadditheen have stated the principle that if someone in the state of kufr heard something from the Prophet ﷺ and then mentioned it after having accepted Islam, it would be accepted, even if it was after the Prophet's ﷺ passing away. If he had accepted Islam during the Prophet's ﷺ mortal life, he would be a companion, and if he had accepted Islam after the Prophet's ﷺ passing away, he would be a Tābi'ee. Shaykh Ahmad Muhammad Shākir writes in Shara Alfiya:

> And as for the one who heard something from the Prophet ﷺ before accepting Islam and then accepted Islam after his passing away, like Tanokhi, the messenger of Hercules, he will be a Tābi'ee. However, his hadith will be Mutassil and not Mursal

77

because regard is given to the narration and he narrated it from the Prophet ﷺ. So even though at the time of hearing it, he was not Muslim, he was at the time of narrating it.

(Shara Alfiya of Suyooti)

Contradicts the Quran

The third possible objection is that this narration is contradictory to the following Quranic verses:

Sura Baqarah describes the condition of those who die in unbelief:

> Their punishment shall not be mitigated. Nor shall they be given respite.   *(Quran 2:162)*

In another place, it states the deeds of an unbeliever:

> And we shall take all that they did and turn into scattered dust.
>   *(Quran 25:23)*

After the Quran has made clear that the deeds of the unbeliever are wasted and there will be no reward for them or reduction in their punishment, how can we accept the narration by Syeduna Abbās for it proves both of these matters for an unbeliever?!

Firstly, one must remember that everyone – even those who oppose the Mawlid gathering – acknowledge the service Abu Tālib rendered to the Prophet ﷺ and that Allah ﷻ reduced his punishment, despite the fact that he died in a state of unbelief. It is written in Sahih Muslim that the Prophet ﷺ was asked:

> Yā Rasoolallah, did you help Abu Tālib in any way because undoubtedly he withstood a lot for you?
> He replied, 'Yes, if it wasn't for me he would be deep down in the fire but because of me only his feet are being burned.'
>   *(Muslim)*

78

Here, this reduction in Abu Tālib's punishment does not contradict the verses[16], so how can the reduction in Abu Lahab's punishment be contradictory? Both are similar in that they refer to dying in a state of unbelief.

Secondly, when the great mufassireen and muhadditheen have made clear that there is no contradiction between this narration and Quranic verses, and have presented reconciliations between the two, there is no scope for any objection. Let us take a look at the statements of universally-accepted muhadditheen who have uprooted such objections and stated that it is a particularity of the Prophet ﷺ that Allah ﷻ showed bounty to even an unbeliever for a deed done for him ﷺ! Hāfiz Ibn Hajar writes:

> This hadith shows that the unbeliever sometimes benefits in Ākhirah from a pious deed, however, this is against the apparent meaning of the Quran where Allah ﷻ said {And we shall take all that they did and turn it into scattered dust} (25:23). This (contradiction) is refuted firstly by the fact that this narration is Mursal because Urwa did not say from whom he heard it. Even if we did accept it as Muttasil, it would still be about a dream, and maybe the viewer of the dream became Muslim afterwards and is thus not proof.
>
> Secondly, even if we did accept it, it is possible that it is specific to the Prophet ﷺ (and not a matter for every unbeliever). The episode of Abu Tālib is evidence of this. As mentioned before, there was a reduction in his punishment because of his service to the Prophet ﷺ, and he was moved from the depths of Hell to the top.
>
> Imām Bayhaqi has said that where it states that the unbeliever's deeds are invalid, it means that the unbeliever will not be saved from Hell and entered into Paradise. However, it is possible for him to attain a reduction in his punishment for all his crimes, other than his kufr. Qādi Iyād has stated there is ijma that an unbeliever's deeds do not benefit him, nor does he receive any blessings or reductions in his punishment, not even a break in

---

[16] Verses (2:162) and (25:23) mentioned above

the punishment. I say that this cannot negate the possibility of what Imām Bayhaqi mentioned, that it relates to kufr, for what is there to prevent reduction in the punishment for sins other than kufr?

Imām Qurtubi stated that the reduction in punishment is specific to Abu Lahab and all those about whom there is scriptural evidence (i.e. it is not for every unbeliever). Ibn Muneer has written in the Hāshiya that there are two issues here, one is that one acknowledges the obedience of the unbelievers, but this is impossible as to be obedient one must have the correct purpose[17], a condition which cannot be found in an unbeliever. The second is that an unbeliever benefits from a deed only through the Bounty of Allah ﷻ. The mind does not deem this impossible. Now that these principles are clear, one should know that even though Abu Lahab's freeing of Thowbiya was not an accepted form of obedience (because of his unbelief), through His *fadhl,* Allah ﷻ reduced his punishment, just as he showed *fadhl* in the matter of Abu Tālib. We are bound by Shariah in terms of accepting or not accepting the punishment (we do not use our intellect); I say that the result of Ibn Muneer's statement is that the stated *fadhl* of Allah ﷻ was in the honour of that blessed entity for whom the unbeliever undertook the good deed (i.e. the *fadhl* is in honour of the Prophet ﷺ and not the unbeliever).

Imām Badr ud dīn Aini has said the same but with an addition:

And this hadith makes clear the matter that even an unbeliever sometimes is rewarded for deeds that are considered good by the people of imān, such as in the case of Abu Tālib. The reduction for Abu Lahab is less than for Abu Tālib because Abu Tālib helped the messenger of Allah and withstood pain for him, whereas Abu Lahab had enmity for him.

(Umda tul Qāri)

---

[17] The correct purpose being that the deed is being undertaken for Allah ﷻ, which only a believer would possess.

Here, it is also worth mentioning the muhadditheen's use of this narration as evidence of the mawlid gathering and to reveal that for them, this narration does in no way contradict Quranic verses. If it did, they would have rejected and not used it. Shaykh ul Qur'a Hāfiz Shams ud dīn Ibn Al Jazari, in his *Arf ut ta'rīf bi Mawlid al Sharīf,* writes:

> So when the unbeliever Abu Lahab, whose condemnation is revealed in the Quran, has his punishment reduced because of his joy on the night of the Prophet's ﷺ birth, what will be the state of the Muslim *muwahhid* from the ummah of Muhammad who also rejoices over his birth? By Allah, the reward for such a Muslim is nothing short of Allah ﷻ entering him into Paradise through His grace. *(Hujja tullāhi alal ālameen)*

The Hāfiz of Shām, Shams ud dīn Muhammad bin Nāsir ud dīn Damishqi, eloquently points out:

> It is authenticated that Abu Lahab has his punishment of Fire lightened every Monday for freeing Thowbiya in happiness at the Prophet's ﷺ birth. (He then wrote the following verses):
>
> 'When an unbeliever, in whose condemnation
> Came (Sura) *'Tabat ya dā'*, who will be in Hell forever
> Verily has his punishment lightened every Monday
> For expressing happiness at the Prophet's ﷺ birth
> What do you think of the servant who, his whole life,
> Rejoiced over the birth and died a believer?!'
> *(Hujja tullāhi alal ālameen)*

Hāfiz Ibn Qayyim also accepts the reduction in punishment and writes:

> And when the Prophet ﷺ was born, Thowbiya gave the good news to Abu Lahab, who was her master, by saying, 'Verily a son has been born to Abdullah this night', so he freed her in happiness and Allah ﷻ did not let that act go to waste for him; after his death he is given water through his thumbs. *(Tohfa tul mowdud bi ahkām il mowlud)*

81

Molāna Abdul Hay Lakhnavi writes:

> So when, because of his happiness at the Prophet's ﷺ birth, the punishment is reduced for an unbeliever like Abu Lahab, why would one from his ummah, who out of love rejoices and spends to his ability, not attain a higher rank?!
>
> *(Fatāwa Abdul Hayy)*

Abu Lahab did not free her at that time

The fourth objection to this narration is that it is wrong to claim that Abu Lahab freed Thowbiya at the time of the Prophet's ﷺ birth, for as the chroniclers of sīra have stated, she was freed after the migration.

The response to this is that there are, without a doubt, three different views amongst the chroniclers of Sīra. Just as some have stated that she was freed after the migration, others stated that Abu Lahab freed her well before the Prophet's ﷺ birth. However, the most authentic and prominent view is that she was freed at the time of the birth. Have a look at the views of three famous chroniclers:

Hāfiz Ibn Katheer mentions Thowbiya being freed and Abu Lahab's reward for it in the following words:

> When Thowbiya gave him news of the Prophet's ﷺ birth, he freed her at that time and was rewarded for it.
>
> *(Al bidāya)*

The words of Hāfiz Ibn Qayyim have been mentioned before but take a closer look at them again:

> And when the Prophet ﷺ was born, Thowbiya gave the good news to Abu Lahab, who was her master, by saying, 'Verily a son has been born to Abdullah this night'. He then freed her with happiness.'
>
> *(Tohfa tul mowdud bi ahkām il mowlud)*

Look at the words of Shaykh Nawāb Siddiq Hasan Qanooji:

Eight women fostered the Prophet ﷺ. His mother did for three, seven or eight days, then Thowbiya Aslamiya, the slave girl who belonged to Abu Lahab, who he freed upon hearing the good news of the Prophet's ﷺ birth.

(As shamāma tul Ambariya)

The second point is that the care and consideration taken by the muhadditheen when narrating was much stricter than the chroniclers of sīra, so when Bukhāri and other books of hadith state that she was freed at the time of the birth, they must be given priority.

The third point is that the muhaqiqeen have also clarified that the authentic position is that she was freed at the time of the Prophet's ﷺ birth. The other two statements are weak. The chronicler of Sīra Shāmiya, Shaykh Muhammad bin Yusuf Sālihi, quotes the writer of Al Garrar:

There is disagreement over when she was freed; it is said that she was freed upon the good news of the Prophet's ﷺ birth and this is sahih. It is also said that Syeda Khadijah asked Abu Lahab to sell her so she could free her but he refused. Then after the Prophet ﷺ migrated to Madīnah, he freed her. This is weak (opinion).

Appendix 2:

List of writings on the Mawlid

A brief list of some writings of the ulema praising and describing the Mawlid:

Husn ul Maqsid fi amal il Mawlid *Imam Jalāl ud dīn Suyooti*

Juz an fil Mawlid as Shareef *Imam Sakhāwi*

Al Mawrid ar Rawā fi'l Mawlid an Nabawi *Mulla Ali al Qāri*

Mawlid an Nabi *Hāfiz Ibn Katheer*

Al Mawrid al Hani fi'l Mawlid an Nabi *Hāfiz Irāqi*

Jāme ul Āthār fi Mawlid an Nabi al Mukhtār
Hāfiz Nāsir ud dīn Damishqi

Arf ut Ta'rīf bi'l Mawlid as Sharīf *Imam Sham ud dīn Al Jowzi*

Al Meelād un Nabawi
Shaykh ul Muhadditheen Imam Ibn al Jowzee (d.597)

Mawrid as Sāwi fi Mawlid al Hādi
Hāfiz Shams ud dīn Damishqi

Al Bāith ala Inkār al Bid'a wa'l Hawādith
Imam Abu Shāma (d.665)

At Tanweer fi Mawlid as Sirāj al Muneer
Imam Abu'l Khitāb Ibn Dahiyya

Nazm el Badee' fi Mawlid an Nabi as Shafee'
Imam Yusuf bin Ismaeel Nibhāni

Hawl ul Ihtifāl bi'l Mawlid an Nabawi as Shareef
Shaykh Muhammad Alawi Maliki

Mawlid an Nabi   *Shaykh As Sayyid Ja'far al Barzanji*

Mā Thabata bi Sunna   *Shah Abd al Haq Muhaddith ad Dehlvi*

Simt ad Durrar fi Akhbār Mawlid Khair ul Bashr
Imam Ali bin Muhammad Al Habshi

Mawlid ul Gharb   *Shaykh Muhammad al Gharb*

Mawlid al Mustafa   *Ustādh Khair ud dīn Dā'ili*

Subl ul Hudā wa'r Rishād   *Imam Muhammad bin Yusuf Sālihi Shāmi*

Faisla Haft Masala   *Hāji Imdād ullah Muhājir Makki*

Saeed ul Biyān Fi Mawlid Sayyid al Ins wal Jān
Shah Ahmad Saeed Dehlvi (d.1277)

Ithbāt ul Mawlid wal qiyām   *Shah Ahmad Saeed Dehlvi (d.1277)*

Khair ul Biyān min al Muhsināt Saeed al biyān fi Mawlid
Sayyid al Ins wal Jān Shah Muhiyy ud dīn Abdullah Abu'l Khair

Khair ul Mawrid fi Ihtifāl il Mawlid
Shah Abu'l Hassan Zaid Farooqi

Ishbā' ul kalām fi ithbāt il Mawlid wa'l Qiyām
Molāna Salāmat ullah Badāyuni

Ad Dur ul Munazzam fi Biyān Hukm Mawlid an Nabi al A'zam
Molāna Abd al Haq Alā Abādi

85

Anwār us Sāti'a dar biyān Mowlud wa Fātiha
Molāna Abd us Samee' Rāmpuri

As Shamāma tul Ambariya min Khair il Mawlid al Bariyya
Allāma Muhammad Siddiq Hasan Khan Bhopāli